Hone,
65, Normanston Drive

# HARMONY

*By the same author*

# HARMONY

A TEXT BOOK FOR CLASS USE,
ON AURAL FOUNDATIONS

BY

## ANNIE O. WARBURTON,

MUS.D., L.R.A.M., A.R.C.M.

1724

**LONGMANS**

LONGMANS, GREEN AND CO LTD
48, Grosvenor Street, London W.1.
*Associated companies, branches and representatives*
*throughout the world*

*First published* 1938
*New impressions by Novographic Process*
1944, 1946, 1947, 1948, *and* 1950
*New edition* 1952
*New impressions* 1954, 1955, 1958, 1961
1964, 1966

PRINTED IN HONG KONG
BY DAI NIPPON PRINTING CO. (INTERNATIONAL) LTD.

# PREFACE

I HAVE noticed that when a large building is being constructed, there is nothing to be seen for a long time except wooden hoardings round the area. Then, all of a sudden, the edifice takes shape, shoots up, and is quickly completed. That is because the foundations take an enormous amount of work and time. And if they are not sound, the whole super-structure will tumble down. It is precisely so in laying the foundations of harmony. It takes a child some time to learn to talk, and longer still to write. Yet many students still write harmony exercises without the faintest notion as to what they sound like or mean. If Dr. Warburton's book moves somewhat slowly, it is because she insists upon pupils knowing what their work sounds like, and what it means. The book is obviously the result of much experience in teaching average beginners, and I know of no book which is so " fool-proof ".

For aural work, Dr. Warburton uses the sol-fa names, and the doh-minor scheme for minor keys. Whatever may be the opinion as to whether " Lah-minor " is preferable to " Doh-minor " or not for the purpose of teaching singers to sight-read, the Doh-minor method is the only possible one for the teaching of harmony.

I heartily commend Dr. Warburton's book for beginners, and especially for class teaching.

C. H. KITSON.

# NOTE TO NEW EDITION (1952)

*Seventh printing*

SINCE this book was written there have been many changes in school examination syllabuses and the new General Certificate of Education has been introduced. No two Examining Boards have the same music syllabus and there are likely to be further changes. Therefore no text book can exactly fit the requirements of all the syllabuses.

This book can however be adapted to fit any syllabus. Some may require the Cadential $\frac{6}{4}$ (and perhaps also the Passing $\frac{6}{4}$) while not requiring a knowledge of the Secondary Triads. It will be found that the chapter on Second Inversions has very little reference to Secondary Triads, and a brief comment by the teacher on the uses of II and VI will make the chapter understandable. The teacher may have to change a note here and there in the exercises or tell the pupil to use II, IIb or VI to harmonise a certain note.

Similarly the root position of the Dominant 7th can be taught without dealing with its inversions. Paragraphs 1—5 and 7—8 of the Dominant 7th chapter can be studied as soon as the root positions of the Primary Triads are known, and the chord in its root position can then be freely used in all future exercises, particularly at the cadences.

VIb and two part writing can be omitted or deferred if wished, and the chapter on melodic decoration can be introduced at any time after the root positions of the Primary Triads are known.

The examination questions given at the end of the original edition have now been deleted as they are out of date, and some additional Rudiments of Music, not covered in Part I, have been put in their place. There is a growing tendency to add Rudiments to the school examination syllabus, and this addition will obviate the need for another text book. The ground for the General Certificate of Education in Music at the Ordinary Level is thus fully covered in this and the author's " Melody Writing and Analysis ", except for the Set Works, which change from year to year.

An Index has also been added at the end of the book.

# CONTENTS

vii

# INTRODUCTION

THIS book has been designed mainly for the use of classes in Secondary Schools, working for the various School Certificate Music Examinations. It can, however, be used by classes in Training Colleges, by candidates preparing for diplomas in music, and by students of any age who are beginning the study of harmony, whether in class or as private students.

The harmony books written by our leading English theorists have been designed mainly for the professional student, who necessarily has a wider background and can proceed much more quickly than a school pupil. This book is designed for the average boy or girl—or for the average beginner of any age. It may be regarded as an introduction to Dr. Kitson's elementary books on Harmony and Counterpoint, and his " Evolution of Harmony ", which are invaluable for more advanced work.

Harmony is considered, by many, to be the main difficulty in the School Certificate music syllabus. The lack of a suitable text book has, however, had much to do with the matter, and it is hoped that this book may meet the need. The study of harmony, on an aural basis, is of great educational value. It is creative, it improves sight playing and it gives an inside understanding of composers' works. Every amateur can benefit greatly from its study, as well as those who intend to make music their career.

The book is planned throughout on an aural basis. To expect every pupil to hear every note he writes is a counsel of perfection, but everything possible is done to help the weak ear. Sol-fa names are used, and chord singing is recommended as an aid to aural recognition. Examples given in the text, and exercises that have been worked on the board should frequently be sung. A class of girls can generally sing the soprano, alto, and tenor parts while the teacher plays the bass. In addition, however, a few examples arranged for equal voices are given when each new chord is learnt, so that the complete chords can be sung by either male or female voices only.

A few ear tests are given, though more will be required. From these models, however, the teacher can see how to make up his own. Ear tests given here may also be used as further examples for illustration in class, or for playing by the pupil at home.

Any new matter is first dealt with aurally. As the pupil generally discovers the reasons for rules for himself, he is not restive at having to obey them.

In referring to chords, Roman Numerals are used instead of technical names, as they are so much shorter. *e.g.*, I = Tonic Triad ; V Dominant Triad, etc. For the same reason sol-fa names are used instead of technical names, in referring to individual melodic parts. *e.g.*, doh – tonic ; te = leading note. Technical and sol-fa names are thought of as being interchangeable in both major and minor keys, so this means that " doh minor " names are used, and the same name always applies to the same effect. The sol-fa names can then be applied throughout harmony teaching without confusion, *e.g.*, in the dominant 7th, te rises and fah falls in both major and minor key. It is believed that the majority of teachers who apply sol-fa names to harmony teaching will approve of this method.

Teachers will hold different views about the amount of keyboard harmony, if any, that can be taught under school conditions. It depends considerably on the size of the class. This book is so arranged, that the earliest chapters can be worked entirely at the keyboard, or entirely in writing, or as a mixture of both, at the discretion of the teacher. No keyboard work is mentioned later in the book, though it can be continued if desired. Students in Training Colleges and those preparing for musical diplomas are strongly advised to continue the keyboard work throughout.

The first harmony chapters divide the work into easy stages (see the chapter headings of Part II) and plenty of easy exercises are given. The teacher must decide whether the pupil needs to work through them all.

Each chord is treated separately and emphasis is laid on

the more ordinary progressions. The average pupil will not manage to use the others musically, and the gifted pupil can quite well learn to use them afterwards.

It is believed that this is the first harmony book to show the pupil how to think, and how to work, stage by stage. This should greatly ease the path of the teacher and pupil.

A list of rules is given in the Appendix, and a smaller list of new ones at the end of each chapter. Notes on harmonic progressions and on methods of working are also included in the Appendix.

Harmony questions from previous School Certificate papers of the various Boards, and from Teachers' Certificate Examinations, given in the Appendix, should also prove useful.

Not every pupil will need to start at the beginning. Some will have had a good groundwork in Aural Training, and will already know most of Part I, and the first chapter or two of Part II ; others may have only a sketchy background. But all should have sound foundations before proceeding further, and these early chapters may well be used for revision purposes, by those who have already done the work.

Parts I and II are meant to be worked side by side. The first chapters of Part II should be begun at once if major scales are known. Intervals must be studied before Chapter IV of Part II, and triads begun (though not necessarily finished) before Chapter VIII of Part II. The minor scale chapters of both parts should be worked together. The best plan is for Part I to be studied in aural lessons, while Part II is being studied in harmony lessons.

The opportunity is taken in the chapter on Triads to explain about Inversions, and to make a few comments on their use in free creative work, as otherwise a long time elapses before a pupil is able to use such a common progression as Ic V. The dominant 7th is also mentioned here for the same reason. But all this can be left till later, if the teacher wishes.

The chords of the minor key are generally treated separately, so that the pupil shall be as sure of minor key progressions as of major.

The first inversions of the Primary Triads are introduced before Secondary Triads, as it is easier to use inversions when there is not a big vocabulary, and there is more chance that pupils will use them freely.

Two part writing is not introduced until the pupil has a fair harmonic vocabulary. It is then treated as free counterpoint on a harmonic basis. If this is not done the average student may write very unmusically.

Unessential notes and discords are treated in a separate section when the pupil is ready to understand them. A preliminary chapter gives a brief description of *all* types of melodic decoration. This should be useful as general knowledge, and should help in the study and analysis of the classics. The simpler types of decoration are then used in two part and four part writing. In the following chapters essential discords are shown as a historical growth from unessential discords. If the teacher does not wish to teach the use of unessential notes (one School Certificate Examining Body does not require them), it is suggested that he takes Part IV, Chapter I Melodic Decoration with his class, for the sake of general knowledge, but omits Chapters II— IV of Part IV. In order to make this arrangement possible there are exercises which do not require knowledge of decoration, in addition to more florid ones, in the later chapters.

Less usual chords and progressions, and modulation, are briefly dealt with in a separate section, Part V. School Certificate candidates should not attempt this section unless their regulations require it, as it adds considerably to the difficulties.

Teaching harmony to a class has many advantages over teaching it to individual pupils. The members of a class can sing exercises together in parts, and they can learn from each other's mistakes. If the class is small enough it is a good plan to begin a lesson by correcting the homework with the class round the piano. New chords may also be introduced in this way. But the bulk of the lesson should take place with the teacher at the blackboard and the class in desks. The teacher should frequently turn to the piano for illustration, however, and there should be plenty of chord and exercise singing. *Everything* should be illustrated at the blackboard, as the visual sense helps the aural sense and the intellectual understanding so much. The class can see chords and exercises take shape under their eyes, and thus see how to work themselves.

In working exercises on the blackboard, members of the class should be asked to work a chord in turn (the teacher writing) and the question and answer form of teaching should very largely be used, so as to be sure that the pupils are thinking of the right thing at the right time. This is very stimulating, and pupils eagerly follow each other's working, and are ready to make comments or point out mistakes.

The use of small dummy keyboards will be found of great value. While one pupil is playing a scale, interval, chord or chord progression the rest of the class can be finding it on the dummy.

It is hoped that the book will stimulate harmony teaching in Schools, and that, wherever it is used, it will make the path easy for both teacher and pupil.

The author gratefully acknowledges the valuable help and advice given by Dr. Kitson, Miss M. Donington, A.R.A.M., Miss L. E. Walter, B.Sc., M.B.E., formerly H.M.I. of Schools, Miss C. M. Martin, M.A., Miss Freda Smith, B.A., L.R.A.M., and Mr. R. H. Hawkins, B.A., M.Ed., and wishes to place on record her great debt to her Head Mistress, Miss M. G. Clarke, M.A., without whose encouragement this book would never have been written.

# PART I

# RUDIMENTS ESSENTIAL TO HARMONY

## CHAPTER I.

### THE MAJOR SCALE AND MAJOR KEYS

(To be studied concurrently with Part II, Chapters I & II)

1 TONALITY. Tonality is the feeling of relationship that exists between musical sounds, both melodic and harmonic, and it is therefore the foundation of Melody and Harmony. If sounds had no ordered relationship to each other music would sound formless and nonsensical.

2 SCALES. The sounds heard in any particular piece of music can be arranged in the order of a scale. The first step in musicianship is to be conscious aurally of the different " colour " of each sound and of the relationship of each one to the keynote and to the other sounds. The " colour " of a sound can be appreciably changed by its rhythmic, melodic, and harmonic context, but it cannot sound like one of the other sounds. It still preserves its individuality. If you have attended an aural class you will already be aware of the mental effects of different sounds. We shall, however, go into the matter more fully when dealing with particular scales.

Many forms of scale have been used as the basis of melody, but the two in most common use to-day are the major and minor. In both scales it is the unequal arrangement of tones and semitones that gives each sound its distinctive tonal effect and feeling of relationship to the other sounds. If all the sounds were the same distance apart they could have no individuality. Play a scale entirely in tones, and you will feel that it has no beginning or ending, and that no note is stronger than another.

3 THE MAJOR SCALE. This consists of eight sounds in alphabetical order, with a semitone between the 3rd and 4th, and 7th and 8th, and a tone between the other steps or

1

degrees. It can be divided into two halves of the same shape called tetrachords.

**Fig. 1**

Notice that if it begins on C no black notes are required on the piano, as the white notes make semitones just where they are wanted.

4 TECHNICAL (OR DEGREE) NAMES. Every step or degree of the scale has a technical name, viz :—

    1 Tonic (the strongest sound, the keynote.)

    2 Supertonic (the note above the tonic.)

    3 Mediant. (Half way between the tonic and dominant when ascending).

    4 Subdominant. (A fifth *below* the tonic, *i.e.*, the lower dominant.)

    5 Dominant. (A fifth *above* the tonic, dominating sound.)

    6 Submediant. (Half way between the tonic and the subdominant when descending, *i.e.*, the lower mediant.)

    7 The leading note. (Generally leads up to the tonic.)

**Fig. 2**

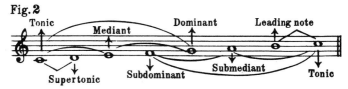

As these names are regularly used by musicians they must be memorised. But they are cumbersome, and another set of names—sol-fa—is much easier for general use.

5 SOL-FA NAMES. These are, in order, for the major scale, doh ray me fah soh lah te doh'. If we are to think musically, a set of names to express *relationship* (as distinct from fixed or absolute pitch names, A B C D E F G) is essential, and as the sol-fa names can be said and thought of much more

quickly than the technical names, they will be regularly used throughout this book.

6 MENTAL EFFECT. As already mentioned, each one of these sounds has its own individuality and feeling of relationship to the other sounds. Notice that doh, me, soh (the tonic tones) feel more stationary than ray, fah, lah, te (the non-tonic tones). Notice particularly the tendency of fah to move to me, and te to move to doh.

A musical realisation of the effect of each sol-fa sound is a big step towards the writing of good melody and good harmony, and must be cultivated assiduously. If you have not had plenty of melodic aural tests in the past you should get all the practice possible now. You must think in sol-fa all the time if you want your ear to improve. Do not be satisfied until you can hear correctly the notes of any simple melody.

7 DIATONIC AND CHROMATIC SOUNDS. The sounds of the key are called " diatonic ", and the scale is called a diatonic scale, whether it is major or minor. The sounds not belonging to the key are called " chromatic ". In sol-fa when a sound is sharpened its name is changed, so that it ends with " e " ; when it is flattened its name ends with " aw ". Usually notes are sharpened going up and flattened going down. Here is the complete chromatic scale in sol-fa : ascending, doh, de, ray, re, me, fah, fe, soh, se, lah, le, te, doh' ; descending, doh', te, taw, lah, law, soh, saw, fah, me, maw, ray, raw, doh.

8 KEYS. A major scale can start on any sound. The scale takes its name from its first sound. If a scale is started first on one sound, then on another, it is said to have been " transposed "

**Exercise I.** Play major scales on the piano starting at different pitches. One octave is sufficient. They must be built up by tones and semitones in the correct order, and the name of the note must be sung or said as it is played. Remember that there must be one, and one only, of every letter name, *e.g.*, D♯, F♯, F♯, not D♯, F, F♯.

9 TRANSPOSITION BY TETRACHORDS, UPWARDS. The top tetrachord of one key can become the bottom one of another,

and the addition of another tetrachord of the same shape produces a key with only one sound different from those of the original key.

**Fig. 3**

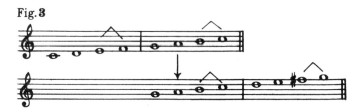

These keys are therefore " closely related ". Notice that key G is much more like key C than key C♯, although C♯ is nearer in pitch.

10 MODULATION.   It sounds very natural for music in the key of C to move to the key of G, as only one sound has to be changed.   Here is part of a well-known tune " Polly Oliver " in key C.   At the end of the second phrase you will feel that G has become doh.   Play the tune twice, first moving to the key of G, and then to key C♯, as shown in the example.   You will hear how unnatural it sounds the second time.

**Fig. 4**   POLLY OLIVER

A change of key in the course of a piece is called " Modulation ", and is one of the best and most usual ways of creating interest and variety in music. There are many modulations possible, some more closely related to the original key than others, and they all have their own peculiar tonal effect. The relationship of keys to each other is another aspect of tonality.

11 MODULATION TO THE DOMINANT. In modulation from the key of C to the key of G, F♯ is used. If this is expressed in sol-fa it is true, from whatever key we start. Therefore learn this rule : In modulation to the soh key, fah is changed into fe and becomes te of the new key.

12 CYCLE OF MAJOR KEYS. (TRANSPOSITION TO DOMINANT.) By building a new scale from the old, as shown in Fig. 3, and continuing the process, we get a complete cycle of major keys from C to C, though the names of the sounds have to be changed from sharps to flats " enharmonically " (*i.e.*, change of name, but not of sound) about half way through, to avoid the use of double sharps.

**Exercise II.** Play one octave of the scale of C, left hand the first tetrachord, right hand the second, keeping all the notes down. Then play the scale of G by repeating the top tetrachord of C with the left hand, and adding another the same shape with the right. Continue through the keys until you get back to C. Say the pitch name of every sound as you play it, making an enharmonic change half way through the cycle. (With a class each pupil can play a key in turn.)

**Exercise III.** Write the cycle of major keys (without signature). Mark the semitones in every scale.

**Exercise IV.** Sing the cycle of major keys to pitch names, changing the names enharmonically half way through. Because of the limitations of vocal range all the scales should be sung between middle C and the octave above, as in Fig. 5.

**Fig. 5**

**Exercise V.** Write the following major scales (without signatures). Mark the semitones : (1) A ; (2) C♯ ; (3) F ; (4) B ; (5) A♭ ; (6) B♭ ; (7) D ; (8) D♭ ; (9) F♯ ; (10) E.

**Exercise VI.** Sing scales as in Exercise IV, but at a command from the teacher stop on a note, give it a new name and continue in the new key. (This exercise may be deferred till later.)

13 TRANSPOSITION BY TETRACHORDS, DOWNWARDS. The bottom tetrachord of one key can become the top tetrachord of another, and the addition of another tetrachord of the same shape produces another " related " key with only one sound different from those of the original key.

**Fig. 6**

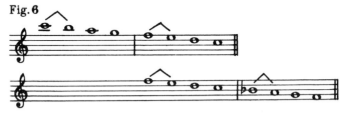

14 MODULATION TO THE SUBDOMINANT. In modulation from the key of C to the key of F, B♭ is used. Therefore learn this rule (true for all keys) : In modulation to the fah key, te is changed into taw, and becomes fah of the new key.

**15** CYCLE OF MAJOR KEYS (TRANSPOSITION TO SUBDOMIN-
ANT). By building a new scale from the old as shown in
Fig. 6 and continuing the process we again get a complete
cycle of keys from C to C.

**Exercise VII.** As Exercise II, but play downwards,
moving to the subdominant key each time.

**Exercise VIII.** As Exercise III, but write the scales
downwards, moving to the subdominant key each time.

**Exercise IX.** Scale Singing as Exercise IV, but modulating to the subdominant key each time.

**16** KEY SIGNATURES. Instead of writing sharps and flats
by each note as required, it is the custom to write them at
the beginning as a " key signature ". As you have already
played and written all the scales, there is no need to write
them out, but here are the signatures for reference :—

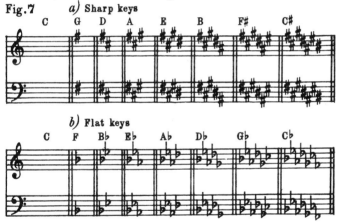

Fig. 7 *a)* Sharp keys

*b)* Flat keys

N.B. 1. The new sharp or flat is always placed last, and
added to the signature of the previous scale. Thus the
sharps and flats are always in the same order.

N.B. 2. Sharps and flats are never put on ledger lines.
Sometimes there are two possible places on the staff, but
custom decrees which one shall be used. In this connection notice particularly the positions of G♯ in the treble,
A♯ in the bass, and F♭ in the bass.

Learn these rules :—

 (1) The last sharp in the signature is te. Doh is therefore a semitone higher.

 (2) The last flat in the signature is fah. The last flat
 but one is doh.

From these rules you will discover the following :—

 (1) How to name a key from the signature :—
  *Sharps.* Doh is a semitone above the last sharp.
  *Flats.* Doh is the last flat but one.

 (2) How to write a signature on being told the key :—
  *Sharps.* Write sharps a 5th above each other,
   starting from F♯, until you come to te.
  *Flats.* Write flats a 4th above each other, starting
   from B♭, until you come to doh ; then
   write one more.

N.B. Exercises X, XI, XII and XIII must be worked
without reference to this book.

**Exercise X.** Write out all the sharp and flat major scales,
with key signatures, in order.

**Exercise XI.** Write the key signatures of the following
major scales, treble and bass : (1) A ; (2) E♭ ; (3) D♭ ;
(4) F♯ ; (5) B ; (6) D ; (7) A♭ ; (8) C♯ ; (9) G♭ ; (10) B♭.

**Exercise XII.** Name the major keys which the following
key signatures represent :—

**Fig.8**

**Exercise XIII.** Name the following notes :—

(1) Mediant of B and E♭ major, (2) submediant of A♭
and G major, (3) subdominant of G♭ and E major, (4)
leading note of C♯ and G♭ major, (5) supertonic of E♭ and
A major, (6) dominant of F♯ and G♭ major.

**17** TRANSPOSITION. As a help towards knowing keys and thinking clearly in them, it is good practice to transpose melodies. In working them at the keyboard play them first in the original key while singing to sol-fa. Then play them in the new key, still singing to sol-fa. The sol-fa names are the link between the two keys. In writing transposition, think in sol-fa also. Plenty of suitable melodies can be found in addition to the graded specimens given below.

**Exercise XIV.** Transpose the following melodies at the piano or in your books :—

Fig. 9

a) to G, D, F, A♭, F♯.

b) to E, B♭, A, F, C♯.

c) to B♭, F, D.

d) to D, A♭, E.

e) to A♭, D, F♯.

## CHAPTER II.

### INTERVALS

(To be studied before Part II, Chapter IV)

1 THE NUMBERING OF INTERVALS. An interval is the difference in pitch between two musical sounds. In numbering intervals both ends are counted. C to D is a 2nd, C to E, a 3rd, etc. If two people sing or play the same note they form a 1st or unison.

2 COMPOUND INTERVALS. Intervals larger than an octave are called Compound, *e.g.*, a 9th is a compound 2nd, a 10th a compound 3rd, etc. In practice, however, C to E is generally called a 3rd no matter how many octaves occur between the notes.

3 MELODIC AND HARMONIC INTERVALS. When the notes of an interval are played or sung one after another, as in a melody, they form a melodic interval. If they are played or sung together, as in Fig. 1, they form a harmonic interval. We shall mostly consider them harmonically in this chapter, as this is a harmony book ; also their effect can be more clearly heard in this way.

4 CONCORD AND DISCORD. Intervals are divided into concords and discords. A concord sounds complete in itself. A discord sounds unfinished and requires a " resolution ". It is not always an ugly sound. Play Fig. 2 :—

(*a*) and (*b*) are both concords, and do not require resolution. (*c*) and (*d*) are discords, but (*c*) is a pleasant one, while (*d*) is harsh.

Play all the intervals from doh in the key of C and decide which are concords and which discords. You will discover that the 1st, 3rd, 5th, 6th and 8ve are concordant, and the 2nd and 7th discordant. The 4th is a strange interval. It sounds discordant if it occurs between the bass and an upper part, or if one of the notes is not a note of the triad. But if it occurs between upper parts and both notes are part of the same triad, then it is concordant. Fig. (3) (*a*) and (*b*) show discordant 4ths with their resolutions. (*c*) shows a concordant 4th.

**Fig. 3**

5 RECOGNITION BY EAR. It is most important to be able to recognise intervals by ear, as they are the foundation of chords. The 3rd should easily be distinguished from the intervals nearest to it, the 2nd and 4th, as it is much softer. Similarly the 6th should easily be distinguished from the 5th and 7th. The 4th and 5th are perhaps the hardest to distinguish from each other. But because the sounds of the 5th blend better, it is harder to hear two separate notes.

EAR TESTS. The teacher should give tests on naming intervals from various notes. In every case the lowest note should be considered as doh for the present and the upper note should be a note of the scale. The pupil should listen for two things : (*a*) the kind of interval, *e.g.*, 5th or 6th ; (*b*) the sol-fa effect of the sounds heard. At first the intervals may be played melodically, but the pupil should accustom himself to hearing the two sounds together. To hear a lower part is the first step in hearing harmony.

6 HEARING BY LOOKING. The ability to hear in your head what you see with your eye is essential if your harmony is to be intelligent and musical. Cultivate this in every way

possible, and never write or analyse anything without doing your best to hear it. After playing the doh chord, try to hear Fig. 4 mentally, then check by playing :—

**Fig. 4**

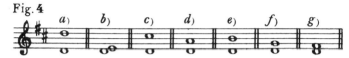

7 RECOGNITION BY SIGHT. The quick recognition of an interval by sight is essential if any speed is to be attained in writing harmony. Try to see quickly, even if you cannot yet hear quickly. Notice that if two notes are on the same staff, they will both be on a line or both be on a space, if they are 3rds, 5ths, or 7ths, whereas one will be on a line and one on a space if they are 2nds, 4ths, 6ths or 8ves.

**Fig. 5**

**Exercise I.** Name the intervals made in Fig. 6 as quickly as possible :—

**Fig. 6**

**Exercise II.** Name the harmonic intervals in Fig. 7 as quickly as possible. (Name *every* interval, there are four in the first complete bar.)

**Fig. 7**

You will later be writing for four voice parts, soprano, alto, tenor, bass (S.A.T.B. for short) thus :—

Fig. 8

(Soprano and tenor notes have their stems up, alto and bass have them down.) Six intervals are made in each chord, viz. : S+A, S+T, S+B, A+T, A+B, and T+B (see Fig. 8 above). You must realise quickly what intervals all these combinations of parts make. Preliminary practice now will make this much easier later. Below is an exercise in naming intervals ; turn to other harmony examples in this book, and name the intervals there also.

**Exercise III.** Name *all* the intervals heard between all the six combinations of parts in Fig. 9. Go right through S and A first, then S and T, etc.

Fig. 9

8 PERFECT AND IMPERFECT INTERVALS. You have heard of Pythagoras. He was a musician as well as a mathematician, and he discovered that a string giving a certain sound will produce a sound an octave higher if divided exactly in half. Therefore he called an 8ve a perfect interval, because the ratio of the vibrating lengths was 1 : 2. Similarly he called the 5th and 4th perfect because their ratios were also low. All other intervals, having a less close relationship to each other, he called imperfect.

1sts, 4ths, 5ths and 8ves are perfect.

2nds, 3rds, 6ths and 7ths are imperfect.

Nowadays we prefer the sound of the imperfect concords, the 3rd and 6th, to the perfect intervals, as they are less bare. But the first people to write harmony in the tenth century thought otherwise. They preferred the pure, bare effect of the 4th and 5th, and they used nothing but perfect intervals ! Here is an example of their music, Organum, as it was called :—

**Fig. 10**

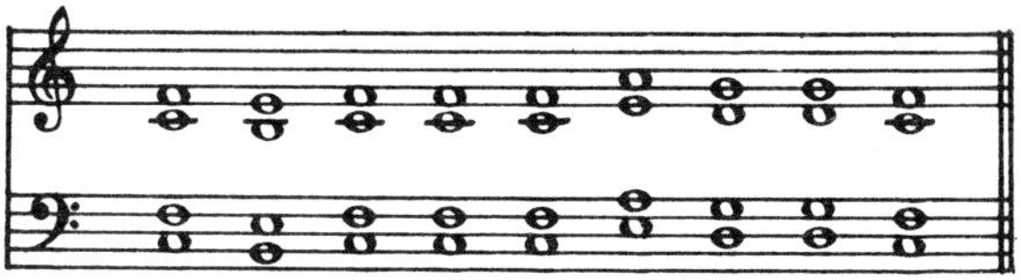

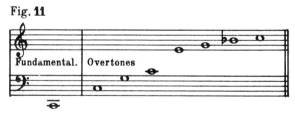

9 THE HARMONIC SERIES. It may interest you to know that scientists have since discovered that when a certain sound is given out, other related sounds vibrate in sympathy. These make what is called the harmonic series. Fig. 11 shows a fundamental sound with its first seven "overtones".

**Fig. 11**

The first intervals are perfect ; then come imperfect concords, and finally discords. The series continues indefinitely, with intervals becoming progressively smaller.

Thus Science has proved that musicians' instinct, in making the triad (root, 3rd and 5th) the basis of harmony, was a good one, as the first five notes of the harmonic series make a triad. When the wind howls in a cave, it is howling a triad !

Have you noticed that a bugle can play only the notes of a triad ? This is because it can blow only the notes of the harmonic series, and in Beethoven's day even horns and trumpets in the orchestra were just as limited. Listen to the horn and trumpet parts next time you listen to a Beethoven Symphony.

10 THE INTERVALS FROM DOH IN A MAJOR SCALE. The 1st, 4th, 5th, and 8ve from doh in a major scale are therefore perfect intervals. The 2nd, 3rd, 6th, and 7th are imperfect intervals. This particular kind of imperfect interval (whether it is a concord like a 3rd, or a discord like a 7th) is called major. In other words all intervals from the tonic of a major scale are perfect or major.

**Exercise IV.** Name the following intervals, giving all the particulars you can (*e.g.*, 5th, perfect, concord ; 3rd, imperfect, major, concord ; 7th, imperfect, major, discord ; etc.). The bottom note is doh in every case.

Fig. 12

11 MODIFICATION OF INTERVALS. When any *perfect* interval is made a semitone larger it is called augmented. When it is made a semitone smaller it is called diminished.

When any *major* interval is made a semitone larger, it, also, is called augmented. But when it is made a semitone smaller it becomes minor, and has to be made a semitone smaller still to become diminished. Thus from a perfect to a diminished interval is one semitone, but from a major to a diminished interval is two semitones. Look at the following plan :—

The perfect interval is so perfect that it comes exactly between augmented and diminished, whereas major and minor share the honours.

12 MORE ABOUT PERFECT AND IMPERFECT INTERVALS. *All* intervals which are not perfect are imperfect. The perfect interval is so perfect that there cannot be various kinds of it. But there are four kinds of imperfect interval : major, minor, diminished and augmented. A diminished 5th is imperfect just as much as a diminished 3rd.

13 EFFECT OF MODIFICATION FROM PERFECT INTERVALS. Play Fig. 13 (*a*). Can you feel that the augmented 4th is a discord, and is pushing outwards as at (*b*) ?

Fig.**13**

Now play Fig. 13 (*c*). The diminished 5th feels discordant also, but much softer than the augmented 4th. It tends to collapse inwards as at (*d*).

(For the sake of completeness, it should be stated here that if the notes making an augmented 4th or diminished 5th are upper notes of a triad the interval, like the interval of a perfect 4th, is treated as a concord. See Fig. 13 (*e*) and (*f*). Other augmented and diminished intervals are always discords, however).

14 THE EFFECT OF MODIFICATION FROM MAJOR INTERVALS. Now play all the major intervals from C and change them into minor, listening for the difference in effect. See Fig. 14 (*a*)—(*d*) :—

Fig.**14**

The minor 2nd sounds even more discordant than the major 2nd, but the minor 7th is softer and less discordant than the major 7th. It is still a discord, however. Do you not feel that it tends to resolve as in Fig. 14 (*e*) ? The minor 3rd and 6th sound just as concordant as the major 3rd and 6th, but different. They tend to sound sadder.

It is possible, of course, for all these major intervals to become augmented and diminished, but these modifications are much less common, and it will shortly be discovered that they cannot occur at all in the major key unless chromatic notes are used. Such intervals as C to E♯, augmented 3rd, and C to E♭♭, diminished 3rd, are more theoretical than practical. But they do exist, and you must not think that C to E♭♭ can be given the same name as C to D because the same notes are used on the piano; a C to a D is always a 2nd, no matter what sharps and flats are used, and a C to an E is always a 3rd.

15 DIFFERENT MENTAL EFFECTS OF INTERVALS OF THE SAME SIZE. Notice also that the same notes on the piano can sound quite different according to the key they are in, and the intervals they make. Play Fig. 15 and notice the effect of the intervals marked *, which are the same on the piano. You will feel that one is diminished and one augmented.

**Fig. 15**

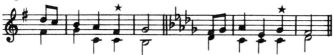

16 MORE ABOUT CONCORDS AND DISCORDS. It should now be clear that all diminished and augmented intervals and all kinds of 2nds and 7ths are discordant. Perfect intervals and major and minor 3rds and 6ths are concords. The exceptions are the perfect and augmented 4th and the diminished 5th which may be concordant or discordant in use.

EAR TESTS. The teacher should play the following intervals after establishing the key, and ask the pupil to name them. The bottom note is always doh. The pupil should think in sol-fa. It is sometimes possible for him to give more than one correct answer—he may hear E♭ to B♮, or E♭ to C♭ (doh to se or doh to law).

**Fig. 16**

**Exercise V.** Modify in as many ways as possible the intervals in Figs. 4 and 12 (all of which are perfect or major). Name the modified interval and try to hear its effect.

17 HOW TO NAME AN INTERVAL FROM ANY NOTE OF THE SCALE. In working exercise V you may have realised that there is an easy way of naming any interval, no matter on what note of the scale it is built. Look at the first interval in Fig. 12. It is a major 6th because it is a 6th from doh. But in whatever key F to D occurs it is still a major 6th. And its augmented form, F to D♯, is an augmented interval in any key.

So in naming an interval, imagine the bottom note as doh, whatever the key happens to be. First name the number of the interval. Then decide whether the top note belongs to the major scale on this doh or not. If it does, then the interval must be major or perfect. If it does not, it is easy to see how much bigger or smaller it is. *e.g.*: (*a*) E to D. Reason as follows : (1) E to D=7 ; (2) 7ths from doh are major ; (3) in the scale of E, D is sharp ; (4) ∴ E to D♯ is a major 7th ; (5) ∴ E to D♮ is a minor 7th. (*b*) F to B. (1) F to B=4 ; (2) 4ths from doh are perfect ; (3) in the scale of F, B is flat ; (4) ∴ F to B♭ is a perfect 4th ; (5) ∴ F to B♮ is an augmented 4th.

**Exercise VI.** Reasoning in this way, name these intervals :—

**Fig. 17**

**Exercise VII.** Write the following intervals : (1) a perfect 4th on A and B♭ ; (2) an augmented 6th on C♯ and G ; (3) a diminished 7th on D and B ; (4) a major 6th on G and F♯ ; (5) a minor 2nd on E♭ and F ; (6) a minor 6th on E and F; (7) a perfect 5th on D♭ and C♯; (8) an augmented 8ve on F♯ and G ; (9) an augmented 7th on C and C♯ ; (10) a minor 6th on B and A♭.

Sometimes you will find an interval awkward to name, built on some note such as A♯, whose scale is not easily thought of. Suppose you have to name A♯ to D♯. It is no solution to turn A♯ into B♭ because that would turn a 4th into a 3rd. So begin by naming A to D♯, augmented 4th. As the interval A♯ to D♯ is a semitone less, it must be a perfect 4th. An interval can be modified by changing the top or the bottom note. But you must always think upwards.

**Exercise VIII.** Name these intervals :—

**Fig. 18**

EAR TESTS. The teacher should now begin to give passages in two parts as ear tests. The pupil, in working these, should not only use his knowledge of the aural effect of the intervals ; he should listen to the movement of each part and feel the sol-fa effect of each note. A few graduated specimens are given here, but many more tests should be given on these lines, in aural lessons.

**Fig. 19**

18 INVERSION OF INTERVALS. When the top and bottom notes of an interval change their relative positions the interval is said to be inverted. In Fig. 20, (*b*) and (*c*) are both inversions of (*a*).

**Fig. 20**

It is useful to know what intervals become when they are inverted. Invert a 1st, 2nd, 3rd, etc., and see what happens. You should get the following table :—

1st inverted become an 8ve $(1+8=9)$.
2nd    ,,          ,,       a   7th $(2+7=9)$.
3rd    ,,          ,,       ,,  6th $(3+6=9)$.
4th    ,,          ,,       ,,  5th $(4+5=9)$.
5th    ,,          ,,       ,,  4th $(5+4=9)$.
6th    ,,          ,,       ,,  3rd $(6+3=9)$.
7th    ,,          ,,       ,,  2nd $(7+2=9)$.

The intervals add up to 9 and not 8, because one note is counted twice, *e.g.*, in C to E and E to C, E is counted twice. So a quick way of finding an inversion is to subtract it from 9.

**Exercise IX.** Name the inversions of the following intervals : 3rd, 7th, 2nd, 4th, 6th, 5th.

You need also to know what *kind* of interval each becomes when it is inverted. Experiment with perfect, major, minor, augmented and diminished intervals. You will discover :—

Perfect     remains   perfect.
Major     becomes   minor.
Minor        ,,     major.
Augmented    ,,     diminished.
Diminished    ,,     augmented.

**Exercise X.** Name the following intervals ; then invert and rename them. Name the inversion from the facts given in para. 18 (*e.g.*, an augmented 5th is bound to become a diminished 4th) and then check by seeing if the notes do make the interval you have stated.

**Fig.21**

**Exercise XI.** Invert and rename all the intervals given in Figs. 12, 16, 17, and 18.

19 ALL POSSIBLE INTERVALS IN A MAJOR SCALE. Now write all the intervals from C in C major, all the intervals from D in C major (*i.e.*, imagining D as doh) and so on, until you have written all the possible intervals in C major. Write the name of each interval above the notes. This is good practice in naming intervals, but it has another purpose, as you will thus discover which intervals can occur in a major scale.

You have discovered plenty of perfect, major and minor intervals. Have you discovered any augmented or diminished ? One, fah to te, an augmented 4th, and its inversion te to fah, a diminished 5th. Remember fah to te. It is an awkward interval and you will hear more about it later. It is sometimes called the tritone because it contains three whole tones.

20 DIATONIC AND CHROMATIC INTERVALS. Intervals which can occur in a diatonic scale (major or minor) are diatonic ; those which can occur only in a chromatic scale are chromatic. You have discovered in para. 19 that an augmented 4th, and its inversion a diminished 5th, are the only augmented and diminished intervals which can occur in a major scale. All other diminished and augmented intervals are

therefore chromatic in a major key. Now think of a semitone. A semitone caused by two notes with different letter names, such as C and D♭, can occur in some major scales and can therefore be a diatonic semitone. But a semitone caused by two notes with the same letter name, such as C and C♯, cannot occur in any diatonic scale major or minor, and is therefore a chromatic semitone.

**Exercise XII.** Define the following terms, as applied to intervals, and give an illustration of each : (*a*) perfect ; (*b*) imperfect ; (*c*) concord ; (*d*) discord ; (*e*) compound ; (*f*) chromatic ; (*g*) diatonic ; (*h*) melodic ; (*i*) harmonic ; (*j*) diatonic and chromatic semitone.

CHAPTER III.

## TRIADS AND THEIR INVERSIONS

(This Chapter can be worked right through immediately
after Intervals, or it can be done in stages at the discretion
of the teacher.

Pars. 1—4 must be studied before Part II, Chapter VIII.
,,   5—10 ,,         ,,         ,,       ,, II,   ,,    X.
,,  11—13 ,,         ,,         ,,       ,, IV,   ,,    V.
Par.  14   ,,         ,,         ,,       ,, IV,   ,,   VI.)

1 DEFINITION OF A TRIAD. A triad consists of a root (*i.e.*,
the note from which the chord is derived), and the 3rd and
5th above it. The 3rd and 5th may be of any kind, so that,
*e.g.*, C E G, C E G♯, C E♭ G♯, C E♭ G♭ are all triads. But
such a triad as C E♭ G♯ cannot occur in any diatonic key,
and in practice there are only four species of triads which
can do so.

2 SPECIES OF TRIADS   These are :—

Major Triad : Root, with a major 3rd and perfect 5th
above it.

Minor Triad : Root, with a minor 3rd and perfect 5th
above it.

Diminished Triad : Root, with a minor 3rd and diminished 5th above it.

Augmented Triad : Root, with a major 3rd and augmented 5th above it.

Fig. 1 (*a*)—(*d*) shows them, built on C :—

Fig.1
a)    b)    c)    d)    e)    f)

As there is only one diminished 5th (te fah) in a major
scale, and no augmented 5th, you will realise that diminished
and augmented triads must be rare. But major and minor

23

triads are so common that they are called " common chords ".

Notice that the rare kinds are called by the name of their 5th, but that as there are two kinds with a perfect 5th they do not use the word " perfect " at all, but take their name from the kind of 3rd they possess.

3 SOUND OF TRIADS. Play Fig. 1 (*a*) and (*b*) again, and compare their sound. They both sound ordinary and concordant, but you can hear the heavier, sadder effect of the minor 3rd.

Now play Fig. 1 (*c*). You can hear that it is a discord. You are used to the effect of the diminished 5th and its tendency to resolve inwards as at Fig. 1 (*e*). Notice that the chord consists of two minor 3rds, one above the other.

Now play Fig. 1 (*d*). Here you have the harsh effect of the discordant augmented 5th. The 5th wants to move upwards as at Fig. 1 (*f*). The two major 3rds, one above the other, are too strong, just as the two minor 3rds in the diminished triad were too weak. The combination of one major and one minor 3rd, as in the major and minor triads, sounds more balanced.

As an augmented 5th cannot occur in a major scale, an augmented triad cannot occur either, so we are not concerned with it for the moment.

EAR TESTS. The teacher may wish to give ear tests on these triads at once, or he may defer them until the triads are linked up with the major scale.

**Exercise I.** Play the chords in Fig. 2 and try to identify them by ear. Then analyse them and write down their names.

**Fig. 2**

**Exercise II.** Write (*a*) major triads on A, B♭ and E ; (*b*) diminished triads on B, C♯ and A♭ ; (*c*) minor triads on D, F♯ and B♭ ; (*d*) augmented triads on D♭, C♯ and A♭.

**4** TRIADS OF THE MAJOR SCALE. Now play all the triads in C major. Name them by ear and then check by analysis. You will discover the following (Fig. 3 (*a*), (*b*) and (*c*)) :—

**Fig. 3**

The Primary Triads, which you are learning in your harmony, are the only major triads in the major key. II, III and VI are minor. VII is diminished and tends to move as at Fig. 3 (*d*), te moving to doh, and fah to me. Look again at Fig. 1 (*e*). Do you see that the resolution you felt by instinct is doing just the same in the key of D♭ major ? As a diminished triad can occur only on te in the major scale, it is easily recognised. Listen for te and fah and their inward resolution.

TRIAD SINGING. Singing triads is the best way of getting to know their sound. Always use sol-fa. Here are some ways of singing them :—

**Fig. 4**

etc., up the scale.

(*a*) As Fig. 4.
(*b*) As Fig. 4, but first sing all the majors, then the minors, then the diminished triads.
(*c*) As Fig. 4, but sing whatever triad your teacher calls out—II, V, etc.

(This exercise should be continuous and the teacher should choose chords that follow well after one another.)

(*a*), (*b*) and (*c*) can then be repeated in the form shown in Fig. 5 (*a*), the class dividing into three parts for the chords.

**Fig. 5**

etc., up the scale.

The teacher can vary these exercises by giving different rhythms, *e.g.*, Fig. 5 (*b*). They should be used frequently, as by their means the pupil gets to know the sound of the triads, without the complications of four-part harmony.

EAR TESTS. The teacher should play a major scale and then an isolated triad from it for the pupil to recognise. The pupil should use sol-fa. He should (*a*) name the chord (II, III, etc.) ; (*b*) name the kind of triad (minor, diminished, etc.) ; (*c*) use the two statements to check each other.

**Exercise III.** Write (*a*) all the major triads in D and A♭ major, the diminished triads in F and F♯ major, (*c*) all the minor triads in E and D♭ major, with key signatures.

**Exercise IV.** Name all the major keys in which the following can occur. (First decide the kind of triad ; if major, then the bottom note can be doh, fah and soh ; if minor, the bottom note can be ray, me, and lah ; if diminished, it can only be te).

Fig. **6**

5 1ST INVERSION OF TRIADS. When the 3rd of the triad is the lowest sound heard instead of the root, the chord is said to be inverted, and in its first inversion. Fig. 7 shows all the first inversions in the key of C :—

Fig. **7**

The chords do not change their names because they are inverted ; they still contain the same notes. But " *b* " is added. *e.g.*, the chords in Fig. 7 are called I*b*, II*b*, III*b*, etc.

6 VISUAL RECOGNITION. The intervals from the bass in the root position are $\frac{5}{3}$, and in the first inversion $\frac{6}{3}$. If they are $\frac{6}{3}$ the root will be a 3rd below the bass note.

Get used to the idea that a root and a bass note are not necessarily the same, and take care to use the words accurately.

Also notice that the word " bass " has two meanings in harmony, viz. : (*a*) bass voice ; (*b*) the lowest part heard, whatever voice or instrument is producing it. *e.g.*, in a part song for female voices the alto is the bass.

**Exercise V.** Name the following chords by Roman numerals, adding " *b* " if they are in their 1st inversion :—

**Fig. 8**

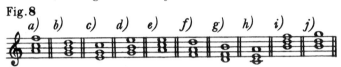

7 AURAL RECOGNITION. If you sing the notes of a first inversion from the top downwards, and then add a 3rd below, you will feel you have come to the root. Do the same with the root position and you will feel the difference ; if you sing correctly you get to a note which does not even belong to the chord. Another method of recognition is to listen for the gap of the 4th in the first inversion (when played three notes in close position).

EAR TESTS. The teacher should now give ear tests in recognising whether a chord is in its root position or 1st inversion.

8 1ST INVERSIONS OF THE MAJOR KEY—Refer to Fig. 7 and play I*b*, IV*b*, V*b*, major first inversions. Then compare them with the sound of II*b*, III*b*, VI*b*, minor first inversions. It is a little harder to tell the difference between major and minor than in the root positions. Notice that the major 1st inversion has a minor 3rd at the bottom and *vice versa*. The best way to recognise them is to hear them in relation to their key and to think of their sol-fa names.

4

Now play VII*b*. Can you feel that VII, when inverted, is no longer discordant ? It can move to several places as in Fig. 9 :—

Fig. **9**

This is because the augmented 4th is sounded between upper notes of the triad. (See Chapter II, para. **13**.)

VII*b* is easy to recognise, because of the presence of te and fah, the augmented 4th.

1ST INVERSION SINGING. Sing 1st inversions in the same ways that you sang the root positions in para. 4.

EAR TESTS. Similar to those given in para. 4 for root positions.

**Exercise VI.** Write I*b*, VII*b*, IV*b*, V*b*, II*b* in the keys of G, A♭, and E major, with key signatures.

**9** 1ST INVERSIONS IN FULLER ARRANGEMENTS. By now you will be familiar with the root positions of the primary triads arranged for the keyboard (Chapters I and II of Part II) and for voice parts (Chapters III—VII of Part II). 1st inversions can be used in a similar manner. You can recognise their sound by the weaker effect of the 3rd at the bottom, and their look by the presence of a 6th from the bass somewhere in the chord, instead of a 5th.

**Exercise VII.** Play the chords given in Fig. 10, and then name them.

Fig. **10**

**10** 1ST INVERSIONS IN HARMONIC PROGRESSIONS. Root positions tend to sound so strong and finished that their continual use gives a very heavy effect.  Cf. Fig. 11 (*b*) with the smoother, more flowing effect of (*a*), and sing the bass of both while the examples are played.  In (*b*) all the chords are in their root position.  In (*a*) the same chords are used, but they are frequently inverted.

**Fig. 11**

THE ASH GROVE

If you attempt free creative work, try to use 1st inversions sometimes.  They give variety and help the rhythm onwards.

But be careful about doubling the bass note (the 3rd). You can write it in 8ves in the bass but it will not generally sound well repeated again in the treble (except in VII*b*). Fig. 12 (*a*) and (*c*) sound better than (*b*) and (*d*). 1st inversions usually sound best when the root is at the top, as in Fig. 12.

Fig. 12

11 2ND INVERSIONS OF TRIADS. When the 5th of the triad is the lowest sound heard, the chord is said to be in its 2nd inversion. Fig. 13 (*a*) shows all the 2nd inversions in the key of C.

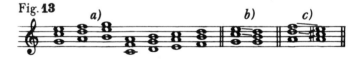

Fig. 13

These are called I*c*, II*c*, etc. The intervals from the bass are $^6_4$. The root is a 5th below the bass note.

12 SOUND OF 2ND INVERSIONS. 2nd inversions are discords. Play the first chord of Fig. 13 (*a*) several times. Do you not feel that it tends to resolve as at (*b*) ? Similarly the 2nd chord, II*c* tends to resolve as at (*c*). Notice that this resolution is out of the key. For this reason II*c* is not normally used.

As 2nd inversions are discords, their use is very restricted. I*c* resolving on V is by far the most common. It occurs so often at a cadence that it is called a " cadential $^6_4$ ". Compare the endings of Fig. 14 (*a*) and (*b*). You will hear how halting I sounds in comparison with I*c*.

Fig. 14

FINALE.– CLOCK SYMPHONY

*a)* *b)* *Haydn*

1st time | 2nd time

Fig. 15 shows some common arrangements for voice parts. The bass note is generally doubled and the other two notes generally move down by step.

Fig. 15 *a)* *b)* *c)*

A 2nd inversion, whether arranged three notes in close position as in Fig. 13 or in a fuller form as in Fig. 15, is easy to recognise because it is a discord, and you can feel its need of resolution.

CHORD SINGING.

Fig. 16 *a)*

*b)* *c)*

EAR TESTS At present a $^6_4$ chord should always be thought of as I*c* going to V. Sol-fa names should be used. The teacher can play the chords as at Fig. 13 or Fig. 15, in isolation, or in a progression, at his own discretion. They are easiest to recognise when part of a cadence progression.

**13** HOW TO USE 2ND INVERSIONS. I*c* V is so common at cadences that you will want to use it very much in free creative work. But do not use any other 2nd inversion, until you know more about them.

**14** THE DOMINANT 7TH. This chord is so frequently used in composition that you will want to know something about it before you come to Part IV, where you learn it thoroughly. It consists of the dominant triad with a 7th from the root added, as at Fig. 17 (*a*).

It is a discord and you will feel that te wants to move to doh and fah to me. Its most usual resolution is on to I. Fig. 17 (*b*), (*c*) and (*d*). show it arranged for four voice parts. It is called ⁷V. As it has four notes, it can have three inversions ⁷V*b*, ⁷V*c*, ⁷V*d*, as at Fig. 17 (*e*), (*f*) and (*g*).

Fig. 18 shows the last three chords of Fig. 11 (*a*)—" The Ash Grove ", with ⁷V in place of V. Cf. the two versions.

In using the dominant 7th in free creative work you had better confine yourself to the use of the root position moving to I at a cadence, until you know more about it.

CHAPTER IV.

## THE MINOR SCALE AND MINOR KEYS

(To be studied concurrently with Part II, Chapters VIII
and IX.)

1 MINOR SCALE FORMATION. There are two scale modes
from which pieces are generally built to-day. One is the
major, the other is the minor. Fig. 1 shows part of a song
in F minor (without key signature) :—

Fig. 1

THE MARSH OF RHUDDLAN

Play it through to hear the general effect, and then write
all the notes it contains, in scale order. You will discover
the following :—

Fig. 2

The semitones occur between the 2nd and 3rd, 5th and 6th
and 7th and 8th degrees and there is an augmented 2nd
between the 6th and 7th degrees.

2 AURAL EFFECT OF THE MINOR SCALE. Fig. 3 (a) and (b)
show C major and C minor. Compare the two.

Fig. 3

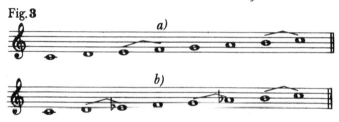

C minor has a flattened 3rd and 6th as compared with C major. So the sol-fa names will be doh ray *maw* fah soh *law* te doh'. Sing the scale to these names.

A major and minor scale starting on the same doh or tonic are called tonic major and tonic minor, in relation to each other.

EAR TESTS. If the mental effects of the minor scale sounds are not already familiar the pupil should be given plenty of ear tests now. Major and tonic minor effects should frequently be compared. Doh maw soh are the restful tonic tones, just as doh me soh are in the major scale ; fah and law often have a tendency to fall, as fah and lah have in the major ; and te has a tendency to rise, as in the major.

The pupil should also be able to recognise aurally whether a piece is in a major or minor key. The minor key generally has a sadder, heavier effect, though not always. A bright rhythm or a quick pace can modify the effect. Tell the pupil to listen particularly for the 3rd of the scale and decide whether it is me or maw, as this is the main distinguishing feature.

**Exercise I.** Play various major scales, then play the tonic minor of each, by flattening the 3rd and 6th degrees. Sing to sol-fa at the same time.

**Exercise II.** Write the following major scales, then write the tonic minor of each by flattening the 3rd and 6th degrees. Use no key signature. Mark the semitones by ∧ and the augmented 2nds by ×. (1) B♭ ; (2) D ; (3) A ; (4) A♭ ; (5) C ; (6) C♯ ; (7) E♭ ; (8) G ; (9) B ; (10) F♯.

3 RELATIVE MAJOR AND MINOR. The minor key most closely related to a given major key is that built on lah, with only one note different, se of the old key.

**Fig. 4**

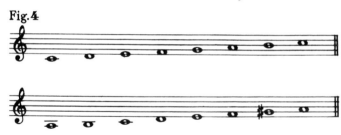

This relationship is expressed by the words relative major and relative minor. *e.g.* :—

C major is the relative major of A minor.

A minor   ,,        ,,    minor of C major.

To find a relative minor from a major call the major tonic doh and move down to lah, *i.e.*, a semitone and then a tone. To find a relative major from a minor, call the minor tonic lah and move up to doh, *i.e.*, a tone and then a semitone.

**Exercise III.** (*a*) Name the relative minor of the following major keys:—(1) B♭; (2) A; (3) C♯; (4) E♭; (5) F; (6) F♯; (7) C; (8) A♭; (9) B; (10) D. (*b*) Name the relative major of the following minor keys:—(1) A; (2) C; (3) B♭; (4) C♯; (5) F; (6) B; (7) A♭; (8) D; (9) F♯; (10) E.

4 MODULATION TO THE RELATIVE MINOR. Fig. 5 shows part of " Come Lasses and Lads ", which begins in C major and modulates to A minor. Play it through, in order to hear the change of doh.

**Fig. 5**

COME LASSES AND LADS

You have already learnt :—

(1) In modulation to the soh key, fah is changed into fe, and becomes te of the new key.

(2) In modulation to the fah key, te is changed into taw and becomes fah of the new key.

Now you can add :—

(3) In modulation to the lah (minor) key, soh is changed into se, and becomes te of the new key.

5 MINOR KEY SIGNATURES. Owing to the peculiar way in which music notation has grown, there is no signature in use which exactly fits a minor key. Think of the notes of C, G and D minor. Their signatures ought to be :—

**Fig. 6**

The above signatures look strange because you have never met them, but aural and notational effects would be much clearer if they were used, and we should know at a glance whether a piece of music was in a major or minor key.

At one time there were many other modes in use besides major and minor, and the feeling for tonality was not as fully developed as it is to-day. So there was no difference of signature for the various modes, and accidentals were put in as they were required.

The result is that, to-day, the minor key, in spite of being quite a separate entity from the major, has no signature of its own, but borrows that of the relative major. See examples in Fig. 7 :—

**Fig. 7**

Notice that, owing to the use of this inaccurate key signature, te requires an accidental ; but remember that it is *not* a chromatic note ; it is diatonic, *i.e.*, part of the key. The notation is misleading.

6 WRITING MINOR SCALES. To write a minor scale with signature, write the signature of its relative major, then write the minor scale from doh to doh, making the 7th note a semitone sharper than it is in the signature. *e.g.*, G minor. (1) Find the relative major of G minor, B♭, and write its signature ; (2) write scale notes up from G to G ; (3) sharpen the 7th note, *i.e.*, make F into F♯ ; (4) Check by seeing if the semitones occur in the right place, or by comparing the scale with that of G major.

**Exercise IV.** Write the following minor scales, with signatures. Mark the semitones and the augmented 2nd : (1) D ; (2) E ; (3) F ; (4) A ; (5) F♯ ; (6) A♭ ; (7) C ; (8) E♭ ; (9) C♯ ; (10) G.

7 CYCLE OF MINOR KEYS. Minor scales form cycles, just as the major scales do. The major signatures can be taken in order, C, G, D, etc., for transposition to dominant, C, F, B♭, etc., for transposition to sub-dominant, and the minor scales which use these signatures, *i.e.*, the relative minors, can be written in this order. They will then make similar transpositions, a minor third lower than the major in each case.

**Exercise V.** Write the minor scale cycles with signatures, making an enharmonic change half way through each cycle. Mark the semitones and the augmented 2nd.

After you have worked Exercise V, you may refer to the following list of signatures. Te is indicated in brackets :—

**Fig. 8**

Exercises VI, VII and VIII should be worked without referring to Fig. 8.

**Exercise VI.** Give the key signatures of the following minor scales and name te in each case : (1) B ; (2) F ; (3) C ; (4) G♯ ; (5) A♭ ; (6) D ; (7) A ; (8) C♯ ; (9) E♭ ; (10) F♯.

**Exercise VII.** Name the minor keys which the following signatures represent. Name te in each case :—

**Fig. 9**

**Exercise VIII.** Name the following notes : (1) Mediant of G and D♭ minor ; (2) supertonic of C♯ and F minor ; (3) leading note of B and B♭ minor ; (4) subdominant of A and D minor ; (5) submediant of B♭ and C minor ; (6) dominant of E♭ and A minor.

**8 HARMONIC AND MELODIC FORMS.** The form of minor scale you have been using so far is used nearly all the time in minor key music and is the basis of minor key harmonies. It is, therefore, called the harmonic minor scale.

But there is also another form in use, called the melodic minor. As used nowadays, it is merely an altered form of the harmonic minor, used in order to avoid an awkward melodic progression. You know that law te makes an augmented 2nd and augmented intervals are rather awkward to sing. So if in a melodic part the 6th and 7th degrees of the scale occur next to each other, lah te is generally used ascending and taw law descending. See Fig. 10 in C minor.

**Fig. 10**

The sounds law and te of the harmonic minor are used for melodic parts most of the time, as it is only when the 6th and 7th degrees occur *together* in a melodic part that the modification is required. Look at the treatment of the 6th and 7th degrees in Fig. 11 :—

**Fig. 11**

Lah and te require sharpening in relation to the signature (see bar 7) ; taw and law require no accidentals, unless lah and te have just been used and require contradicting (see bar 5). Unfortunately, this is all very confusing. When you learnt major keys an accidental meant a chromatic note (or a modulation). In the minor key law, lah, taw and te are all considered diatonic but lah and te require accidentals and taw and law do not. So care is needed when the 6th and 7th degrees of the minor scale occur together. In writing dictation it may be wise to write out the notes soh, lah, te, doh', taw, law, soh on the staff, as at Fig. 10, before starting.

Fig. 12 shows a few melodic minor scales.

EAR TESTS. Plenty of ear tests on the use of the melodic minor should be given if the pupil is not already familiar with it.

**Exercise IX.** Write the melodic form of the following minor scales with signatures : (1) C ; (2) D ; (3) F ; (4) C♯ ; (5) E♭ ; (6) F♯ ; (7) E ; (8) G ; (9) G♯ ; (10) A♭

9 HOW TO TELL WHETHER A PIECE IS MAJOR OR MINOR. A key signature can belong to two keys, a major and a minor, and the signature alone gives no indication as to which of the two the music is in. Yet the person who started to sing or play or write without knowing which it was, would get quite a false conception of the music. *e.g.*, Fig. 13 (*a*) heard in G major (doh ray | me doh te doh | lah) sounds quite different from the same phrase heard in E minor (maw fah | soh maw ray maw | doh). After singing (*a*), imagining it in both keys, play the harmonised versions (*b*) and (*c*), which further accentuate the difference.

**Fig. 13**

Consider the key signature in Fig. 13. It belongs to G
major and E minor. If the piece is in G major it will probably
end with a melody note G, and certainly with a bass note
G and a chord of G. If the piece is in E minor it will end
with a chord of E ; also there will probably be some D♯s
(tes) in the piece and perhaps a few C♯s (lahs) too, if the
melodic minor is used. So there should be no difficulty in
telling whether the key is major or minor.

CHAPTER V.

## INTERVALS AND TRIADS IN THE MINOR KEY

(Like Chapter III this chapter can be worked immediately after the previous one, or parts of it can be deferred till later. The harmonic form of the minor scale is implied throughout the chapter).

1 THE INTERVALS FROM DOH IN A MINOR SCALE. These are the same as in the major, except that doh maw is a minor third, and doh law a minor 6th. Try to hear the intervals of Fig. 1 mentally, then check by playing.

**Fig. 1**

EAR TESTS. The teacher should give ear tests of intervals from doh, in a minor key. (He may, if he wishes, include tests in the melodic minor, but they are not necessary for the harmony of this stage.)

2 ALL POSSIBLE INTERVALS IN A MINOR SCALE. Write and name all the possible intervals in C minor, from C upwards, from D upwards and so on. Put a ring round all that are augmented or diminished. You will discover the following :–

**Fig. 2**

Remember which the augmented intervals are, as you will have to avoid them in melodic parts.

EAR TESTS. The teacher should give ear tests on the intervals of the minor scale, particularly the augmented ones. He should also give two part melodic ear tests, similar to those quoted in Chapter II at the end of para. 17, but in the minor key.

**Exercise I.** Write out all the augmented intervals in the keys of G, B♭, F and C♯ minor.

3 TRIADS OF THE MINOR SCALE. Play all the triads in C minor. Name them by ear and check by analysis. You will discover the following :—

Fig. 3

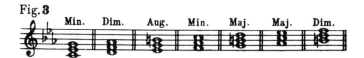

Compare them with the triads of the major scale. Consider the primary triads first. I and IV are now minor, but V is still major, as in the major key. Now consider the secondary triads. VII is still diminished, but so now is II, which was minor in the major key. III which was minor is now augmented, and VI which was minor is now major. II, III and VII are all discords therefore, and are rarely used.

TRIAD SINGING. Sing the triads of the minor scale in the ways shown in Chapter III, para. 4.

EAR TESTS. The teacher should play triads of the minor key. The pupil should name the chord, and also state the kind of triad, using one statement to check the other.

**Exercise II.** Write (*a*) all the major triads in F and E minor ; (*b*) all the diminished triads in D and A♭ minor ; (*c*) all the minor triads in C and F♯ minor ; (*d*) the augmented triads in G and C♯ minor, with key signatures.

**Exercise III.** Name all the minor keys in which the following can occur :—

Fig. 4

4 THE 1ST INVERSIONS OF TRIADS IN A MINOR KEY. Play all the 1st inversions in C minor, as shown in Fig. 5 (*a*).

Fig. 5

You will remember that VII*b* in the major key, the first inversion of a diminished triad, is a concord. The same applies to II*b* and VII*b* in the minor key, and they can be used freely.

The 1st inversion of the augmented triad, III*b* in the minor key, is still a discord, however. Can you feel its tendency to move, as at Fig. 5 (*b*) ?

1st inversions should be sung, and ear tests should be given, as in the major key.

**Exercise IV.** Write I*b*, VI*b*, IV*b*, VII*b*, II*b*, V*b* in the keys of E, B♭, and F♯ minor, with key signatures.

5 THE 2ND INVERSIONS OF TRIADS IN THE MINOR KEY. These are discords, as in the major key, owing to the presence of the 4th from the bass. As in the major key, Ic moving to V at a cadence is the most common. Fig. 6 shows some arrangements of it. The bass note is generally doubled and the other notes move down by step, as in the major.

Fig. 6

ABERYSTWYTH

CHORD SINGING.

Fig. 7

EAR TESTS. The teacher should give ear tests similar to those given in the major key.

6 THE DOMINANT 7TH. This chord is identical in major and minor keys. Te rises and fah falls in the minor as in the major key. Fig. 8 shows some arrangements of the chord and its inversions in C minor, and Fig. 9 shows some arrangements for equal voices.

**Fig. 8**

**Fig. 9**

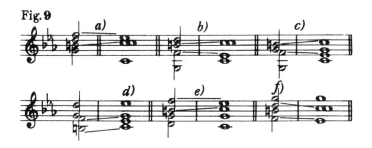

PART II

## THE PRIMARY TRIADS (CONCORDS)

### CHAPTER I.

### I, IV, V MAJOR KEY; ISOLATED CHORDS;
### PIANO ARRANGEMENT

(Major scales should be known before studying this chapter.)

1 CHORDS. A chord is a combination of at least three sounds. Some combinations sound more pleasant than others, and what sounds unpleasant to one generation of musicians may sound pleasant to another. But for over 300 years men have been building up their chords on the same system, extending the harmonic possibilities as time has gone on, yet not altering the fundamental conception.

2 TRIADS. The basis of this system is the triad, *i.e.*, a chord consisting of a root, and a 3rd and 5th above it. The root is the name given to the note from which the chord is derived.

**Fig. 1**

Notice that a triad is built up in 3rds (paradoxically two 3rds make a 5th). Later on you will discover that it is possible to continue adding 3rds upwards, thus making chords of the 7th, 9th, etc. But triads form by far the largest part of most harmony you will meet.

3 THE PRIMARY TRIADS. Some triads are more important than others. The three most important and most frequently used are those built up on the tonic, subdominant and dominant, doh, fah and soh. Fig. 2 shows them in the Key of C major :—

**Fig. 2**

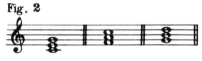

The doh chord consists of doh, me, soh.
The fah chord consists of fah, lah, doh.
The soh chord consists of soh, te, ray.
Learn this thoroughly.

CHORD SINGING. Sing the scale of C, and then sing these chords to sol-fa names, in order to hear their effect. If you are in a class you can sing them in three part harmony. Otherwise you will have to sing them melodically or play them at the piano.

You will probably feel that the doh chord is more finished than the other two, and that the soh chord sounds brighter and less finished than the fah chord, owing largely to the presence of te.

4 NOMENCLATURE. As the tonic chord is built on the 1st note of the scale, the subdominant on the 4th, and the dominant on the 5th, these chords can briefly be called I, IV, and V.

EAR TESTS. The teacher should first establish a key by playing chords or the scale, and then play I, IV, or V as shown in Fig. 2. The pupil should use sol-fa to help identification.

**Exercise I.** Play and write I, IV, and V in various major keys as shown in Fig. 2. Always build the chords upwards from the root, doh, fah or soh, and use sol-fa names all the time. When playing, always begin by playing the scale. Chord playing can be combined with scale playing when piano practice is being done. Listen carefully to the effect.

5 DIFFERENT ARRANGEMENTS OF A TRIAD. Any note of a triad can be used at any octave, and may occur several times. At present the root should be at the bottom but any note can be at the top. Thus, many different arrangements of the same triad are possible, and they will vary according to the medium used—voices, piano, string quartet, orchestra, etc. Fig. 3 shows some possible arrangements of I, key C major, for the piano :—

**Fig. 3**

6 THREE NOTES IN CLOSE POSITION. A very common piano arrangement of a triad is to have the root in the left hand, and a root, 3rd and 5th as close to each other as possible in the right hand. This is known as " close position". Three positions are available, according to whichever note is at the top. The chord always sounds more finished when the root is at the top. Fig. 4 shows I, IV, and V key C major, treated in this way :—

**Fig. 4**

CHORD SINGING. Fig. 5 shows the chords in the same positions, but arranged for equal voices, *i.e.*, all male or female. This and later examples are given so that classes which do not contain mixed voices (*i.e.*, both male and female) may sing chords and hear the effects for themselves. Male voices should sing an 8ve lower than written. When there are mixed voices the ordinary examples shown in the text can be sung. The class should divide up, according to the teacher's instructions, and sing the following :—

**Fig. 5**

EAR TESTS. At this stage the teacher should give three kinds of ear tests, as follows :—

(*a*) Major triads without relation to a key, the pupil to say whether the root, 3rd or 5th is at the top. He must find out whether the top note sounds like doh me or soh.  *e.g.* —

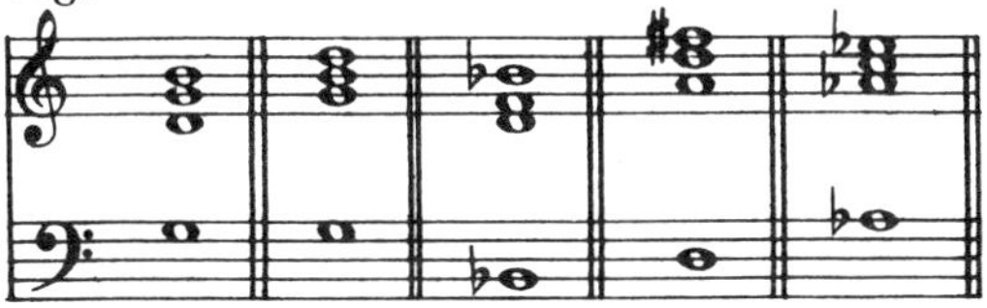

(*b*) I, IV, and V played in isolation after the key has been established, the pupil to say which chord is being played. He must listen to the bass, which will be doh, fah or soh. It must be impressed upon him that the ability to hear and recognise a bass is the hall-mark of a musician. (If he finds difficulty let him sing bass parts while chords are played (*a*) looking at the music ; (*b*) from ear. Examples printed later in this book may be used for the purpose.)

Establish the key and then play chords like the examples given in Fig. 7.

Fig. 7

(*c*) I, IV and V played as in Fig. 7, the pupil to say which note is at the top, in addition to naming the chord. He must first decide what the chord is.

If it is I then the melody note must be doh, me or soh.
If it is IV then the melody note must be fah, lah or doh.
If it is V then the melody note must be soh, te or ray.
One fact checks the other.

7 PLAYING TRIADS IN CLOSE POSITION. Playing triads in close position at the piano will help you to become familiar with them, and to recognise them, providing that you are listening keenly all the time. Work as follows :—

(1) Find the root and play it with the left hand. Keep it down while you are thinking about the next stage.

(2) Looking at your left hand, imagine a triad built on the note you are holding down. There are two things to think about : (*a*) finding a root, 3rd and 5th ; (*b*) realising what accidentals are required in the key concerned. *e.g.*, IV in A major : (*a*) a D, an F, and an A are required ; (*b*) the F has to be sharp.

(3) Play the notes thus found with the right hand. The fifth of the chord will be at the top, as in Fig. 4 (*a*).

(4) Repeat the bass note, and in the right hand transfer the lowest sound an octave higher, keeping the other two where they are. The root of the chord will now be at the top, as in Fig. 4 (*b*).

(5) Repeat the process once more, so that the third is at the top, as in Fig. 4 (*c*).

**Exercise II.** Play I, IV, and V separately in all three positions in various major keys.

8 WRITING TRIADS IN CLOSE POSITION. Work as follows :—
(*a*) Write the Roman numeral under the bass staff.
(*b*) Write the bass note, which *must* be the root.
(*c*) Write the notes in the treble, in close position. Remember to build *up* from the bass ; if you build downwards a different chord is produced.
(*d*) Write the other positions in the same way.

**Exercise III.** Write I, IV and V separately in all three positions in various major keys.

9 HARMONISING ISOLATED MELODY NOTES. Play every note of the major scale, and ask yourself if it can belong to I, IV or. V. You will discover the following :—

Doh can be harmonised by I and IV.
Ray can be harmonised by V.
Me can be harmonised by I.
Fah can be harmonised by IV.
Soh can be harmonised by V and I.
Lah can be harmonised by IV.
Te can be harmonised by V.
Learn this table thoroughly.

Notice that every note of the scale belongs to at least one of the primary triads.

You should now be able to harmonise isolated melody notes. Work as follows :—

(1) Think of the note in sol-fa, and decide to which chord or chords it belongs. If doh or soh is the melody note, two different chords are possible.
(2) Write the Roman numeral under the bass staff.
(3) Write the root in the bass.
(4) Add two notes in close position in the treble, *below* the given melody note. Realise that, though you are now building downwards from the melody, you must think *upwards* from the root to find the right notes.

**Exercise IV.** Harmonise these melody notes, giving two arrangements where possible.

Fig. 8

## CHAPTER II

## I IV AND I V MAJOR KEY WITH BINDING NOTES, PIANO ARRANGEMENT

1 JOINING TRIADS WITH BINDING NOTES. The next stage is to learn to combine chords. There are many possible ways, but we shall begin with the simplest.

In writing simple harmony the aim is always to move as smoothly as possible from note to note, and to stay on the same note where possible, this note acting as a " binding note ".

When I and V are next to each other soh can act as a binding note, as it is common to both chords, and the other notes can move by step. See Fig. 1.

**Fig. 1**

CHORD SINGING.

**Fig. 2**

Similarly I can be joined to IV. This time doh is the binding note. See Fig. 3.

**Fig. 3**

CHORD SINGING.

2 PLAYING TRIADS JOINED WITH BINDING NOTES. Work as follows :—

(1) Find the first chord, first position, as directed in para. 7, Chapter I. Keep it firmly down while you think about the next stage.
(2) Name the notes of the next chord.
(3) Get your finger ready to play the root of the new chord in the left hand, while still keeping the root of the first chord down.
(4) Look at the right hand notes you have down, to see which is the binding note. Notice whether it is at the top, middle or bottom. Keep your finger firmly on this binding note.
(5) See whether the other two notes have to move up or down by step, to get to the new notes required. When you have decided, move both hands at the same time.
(6) Move back to the first chord.
(7) Play the other positions in the same way.

**Exercise I.** Play (a) I VI ; (b) I IVI ; (c) V I ; (d) IV I in various major keys, three notes in the right hand and one in the left, as shown in Figs. 1 and 3, and explained in para. 2.

3 WRITING TRIADS JOINED WITH BINDING NOTES. Work as follows :—

(1) Write the Roman numerals under the bass staff.
(2) Write in the bass notes (*roots*).
(3) Write the treble notes of the first chord in close position, building up from the bass.
(4) Write the treble notes of the second chord in close position, keeping a binding note.
(5) Write the other positions in the same way.

**Exercise II.** Write (a) I V ; (b) I IV ; (c) V I ; (d) IV I ; in various major keys, three notes in the right hand

and one in the left, as shown in Figs. 1 and 3 and explained in para. 3.

EAR TESTS. The teacher should play similar progressions for the pupil to recognise. The pupil should first name the chords, then the melody notes. Melody and bass can be written thus : $\frac{d\ t}{I\ V}$, or on the staff, whichever the teacher prefers. The teacher should establish the key and then play examples similar to the following :—

**Fig. 5**

4 CADENCES. A cadence is the name given to the last melody notes and chords of every phrase. Some cadences are more finished than others. The four types are as follows :—

Perfect     Cadence.  V to I ⎫
Plagal      Cadence.  IV to I ⎬ (Both " Full Closes ").
                              ⎭
Imperfect   Cadence.  Any chord to V (" Half Close ").
Interrupted Cadence.  V to any chord except I, often VI.
Play Fig. 6, noticing their effect.

**Fig. 6**

The perfect cadence sounds brighter than the plagal. Listen for te in V. The imperfect cadence sounds unfinished. Listen for te in the last chord. We expect V I in an interrupted cadence, so the unexpected chord is easily recognised.

Notice that the final chord always occurs on the strong accent.

We cannot yet deal with the interrupted cadence. But the others can now be played, written and recognised.

5 THE PERFECT CADENCE. In order to keep the binding note the melody will have to be ray me, te doh, or soh soh, at present. See Fig. 7.

**Fig. 7**

CADENCE SINGING. Only those singing the two top parts of the chords should sing the melody; the rest should join in at the cadence.

**Fig. 8**

**Exercise III.** Play and write perfect cadences in various major keys.

**6** THE IMPERFECT CADENCE. At present IV cannot be joined to V, as there is no binding note. So the only imperfect cadence that can be made is I V. The melody will have to be soh soh, me ray, or doh te at present. See Fig. 9.

**Fig. 9**

CADENCE SINGING.

**Fig. 10**

**Exercise IV.** Play and write imperfect cadences in various major keys.

7 THE PLAGAL CADENCE. At present the melody will have to be doh doh, fah me, or lah soh. See Fig. 11.

**Fig. 11**

CADENCE SINGING.

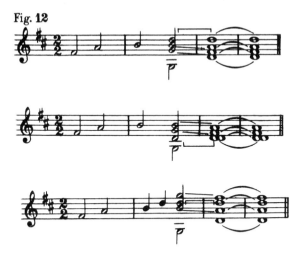

Fig. 12

**Exercise V.** Play and write plagal cadences in various major keys.

EAR TESTS ON RECOGNISING CADENCES. The teacher should now play simple phrases ending with these cadences, for the pupils to name. A few examples are given, but the teacher should improvise many more or find examples from other sources. At this stage there should be no decorations or inverted chords, or anything likely to cause confusion in the mind of the pupil. There should be only one cadence in each test.

Fig. 13   a)

8 HARMONISING MELODY NOTES AT CADENCES. The next stage is to recognise what cadence is implied when the melody is given. At present the last two melody notes must belong to I V, V I or IV I. Work as follows :—

(1) Think in sol-fa and decide to which cadence chords the melody notes belong.

(2) Write the Roman numerals of both chords.

(3) Write the roots of both chords.

(4) Add two notes in close position below the first melody note, thinking upwards from the root.

(5) Fill in the second chord in the same way. Keep a binding note.

**Exercise VI.** Harmonise the last two notes only of the following melodies. State the cadence formed.

**Fig. 14**

9 HARMONISING MELODIES WITH PRIMARY TRIADS. You have already discovered that every note of the scale belongs to at least one of the primary triads (Part II, Chapter I, para. 9). This means that it is possible to harmonise any melody that does not modulate or use chromatic notes with these three chords alone. Many simple melodies of the nursery rhyme, folk dance and song, or sing-song type are harmonised thus. In more advanced music we prefer to use some other chords for variety. Fig. 15 shows a well-known tune harmonised by only the primary triads :—

**Fig. 15**

AULD LANG SYNE

N.B.—Every note is not harmonised, as the accompaniment would be too heavy.

**Exercise VII.**    Harmonise the following fragments of melodies, with a chord for each note.   Work as follows :—

(1) Decide to which chord each melody note can belong, and fill in the Roman numerals.   Do not use the same chord twice together in this exercise, and avoid IV and V next to each other.

(2) Fill in the bass.

(3) Fill in the first chord.

(4) Fill in the second chord, keeping a binding note. Continue in the same way.   Try to hear what you write.

**Fig. 16**

## CHAPTER III.

### WRITING FOR VOICE PARTS. ISOLATED CHORDS

1 VOCAL WRITING. There are many styles of writing for voices, and various numbers of parts are possible, though composers rarely write for more than eight. Sometimes the parts are for equal voices. But the most common combination is four parts for mixed voices, soprano, alto, tenor, and bass, as in most hymn tunes. Your aim, for some time to come, will be to write exercises as much like chants and hymn tunes as possible, though it is hoped you will eventually be able to write for other mediums. There is no reason why you should not continue to experiment for yourself in piano writing (which is more free, and therefore more difficult to do well). You can try to write waltzes, minuets, gavottes and marches, and perhaps songs with piano accompaniment. The book keeps to vocal writing at this stage partly because, being easier, it is required for elementary harmony examinations, and partly because it is the best and simplest way of learning about the movement of chords, and of individual parts, *i.e.*, " part writing ".

2 VOCAL RANGE. Remember that members of a choir have not such a wide range as soloists. If you are a school girl think what the average soprano and alto (contralto) can do in the singing class, and keep to that. The simplest way to remember the range of tenor and bass is to think of these voices as being an octave lower than soprano and alto. If you are a boy then you will know the tenor and bass range and you can think of the soprano and alto as being an octave higher. Keep within the following limits :—

Fig. 1

3 VOCAL ARRANGEMENT. When writing for soprano, alto, tenor, and bass (S.A.T.B. for short) it is customary to write for S. and A. on the treble stave and T. and B. on the bass stave, thus :—

**Fig. 2**

(Notice that S. and T. have their stems up, and A. and B., down.) This is called writing in " short score ". In " open score " the same chords would be arranged thus :—

Fig. **3**

Notice that the tenor uses the treble clef, as it is supposed to be easier to read, and that his notes are written an octave higher than he is singing them. Part songs, choruses from operas and oratorios, and all rather elaborate vocal writing, is written in open score, as it would be too crowded on only two staves. We shall write entirely in short score.

4 DOUBLING NOTES OF THE CHORD. As a triad consists of only three different notes, one note will have to be used twice in four part harmony. Play Fig. 4, and decide which doubling you like best.

**Fig. 4**

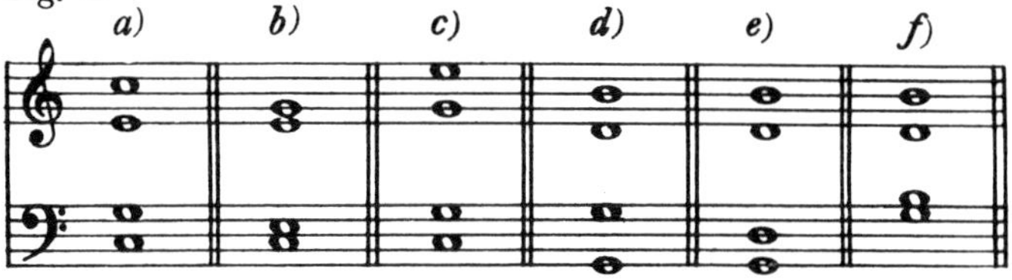

You will probably think that the doubled root sounds best, then the doubled 5th and then the doubled 3rd. But you may feel there is little or no difference, or even prefer the doubled 3rd ! This will be because your ear is not as keenly developed as that of more experienced musicians. Try to develop it so that you can hear the inner parts. *e.g.*, try to hear the difference between the chords in Fig. 5, which have all the notes the same except the tenor. Do you not feel that the doubled 3rd is too heavy ?

**Fig. 5**

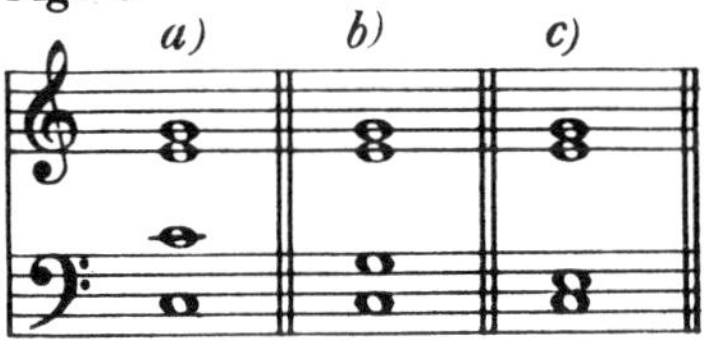

There are cases, of course, where it is good to double the 5th and 3rd, but they will not arise yet, and for the present it is better to double the root.

5 OMITTING NOTES OF THE CHORD. Obviously you cannot omit the root as, at present, it must be in the bass. Now omit the 3rd and 5th and see how you like the effect :—

**Fig. 6**

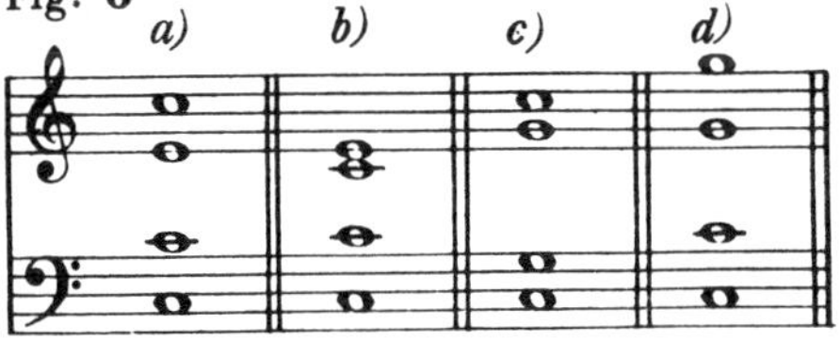

You will probably think that it sounds quite right to omit the 5th and have three roots, but that a chord without a 3rd sounds very bare. So composers avoid doing this unless a special effect is wanted. You will naturally learn how to get ordinary effects first. At present you should almost always have two roots, one 3rd and one 5th, as this arrangement sounds fuller ; but remember that it is possible to have three roots, one 3rd and no 5th.

6 TWO PARTS SINGING A UNISON. This is quite satisfactory, though the chord does not sound as full as it would if the four parts were all singing different notes. Notice how the unison is written.

**Fig. 7**

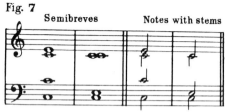

CHORD SINGING. Fig. 8 shows good and bad arrangements. Listen and judge, while you sing.

**Fig. 8**

7 SPACING FOUR VOCAL PARTS. There are many possible ways of spacing voices. Play Fig. 9, listening to the effect. Some arrangements do not lie well for the hands, but this does not matter, as they are vocal arrangements.

**Fig. 9**

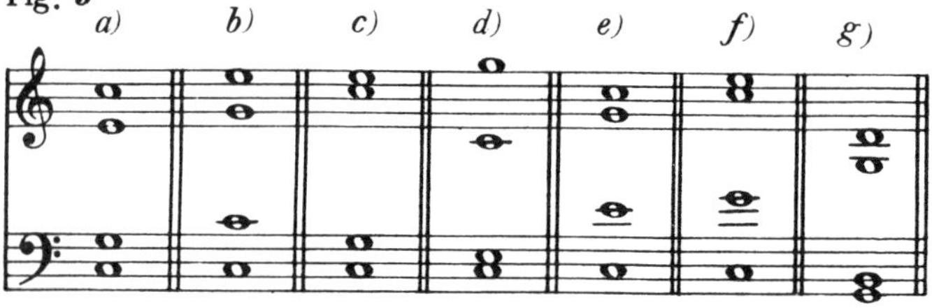

You will discover that (1) parts arranged at about equal distances from each other sound well : (*a*) and (*b*) ; (2) more than an 8ve between adjacent upper parts sounds awkward : (*c*) and (*d*) ; (3) more than an 8ve between the bass and tenor sounds satisfactory : (*e*) and (*f*) ; (4) it is not good to have the tenor too low down, particularly if it is a 3rd from the bass : (*g*). In wide spacing it is often better to have larger intervals at the bottom and smaller intervals at the top of a chord. This follows the principle of the Harmonic Series. (See Part I, Chapter II, Fig. 11.)

Turn to Figs. 3 and 8 in Chapter V for examples of good doubling and spacing.

8 CROSSING OF PARTS. In advanced composition the parts frequently interweave, the tenor perhaps going higher than the alto, or the alto higher than the soprano. But this does not occur in music with simply moving parts such as hymn tunes, as it would cause confusion to the singers and listeners. So do not allow your parts to cross at present.

Fig. 10 shows examples of crossing. (*c*) is part of a hymn tune. There is a danger that listeners, and those singing from ear, will think that the soprano is F, not D, at *

**Fig. 10**

EAR TESTS. The only kind of ear test dealing with the material of this chapter is to recognise differences of doubling and spacing between similar chords. A few tests are included (Figs. 11–13), but they are very difficult, and some teachers may prefer to play the examples while the pupil follows them in the text book.

(1) State which voice part has the 3rd in the following chords :—

Fig. 11

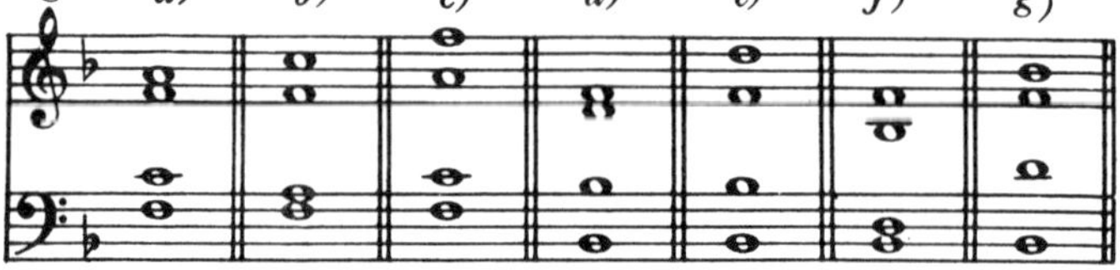

(2) State which note is doubled in the following chords :—

Fig. 12

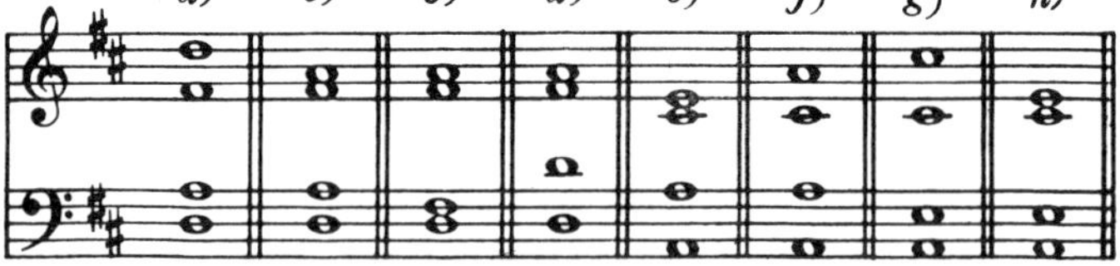

(3) Comment on the spacing of the following chords :—

Fig. 13

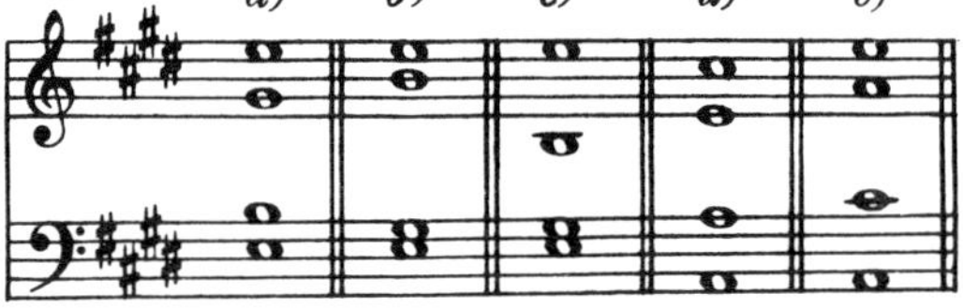

9 ADDING THREE UPPER PARTS TO A BASS NOTE. The method of working can best be explained by an example. You are to write three upper parts above the bass note E in Fig. 14 (a).

**Fig. 14**

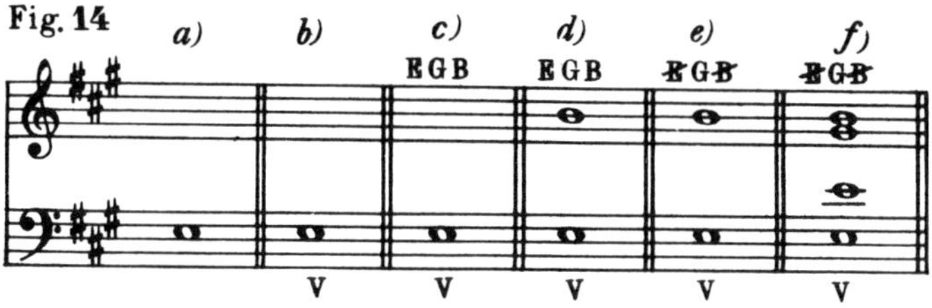

(1) Write the Roman numeral under the bass. Fig. 14 (*b*).
(2) Write the names of the notes required above the treble. Fig. 14 (*c*).
(3) Choose a melody note. Fig. 14 (*d*).
(4) Cross out the names of the notes you already have. Fig. 14 (*e*).
(5) Say to yourself : We have an E and a B. We want another E and a G.
(6) Put the E and G in alto and tenor so that the spacing is satisfactory. Fig. 14 (*f*).
(7) Check, to be sure that spacing and doubling are satisfactory.
(8) Try to hear what you have written.
(9) Check the sound by singing or playing, or both.

This may seem a long way round, but it is the right order of thinking and working. It will rapidly get quicker, and in time become automatic, but you should go through all the stages at present.

**Exercise I.** Write four good arrangements for S.A.T. over each bass note in Fig. 15.

**Fig. 15**

10 ADDING THREE LOWER PARTS TO A MELODY NOTE. The method of working can again best be explained by an example. You are to write three lower parts below the soprano B♭ in Fig. 16 (*a*).

**Fig. 16**

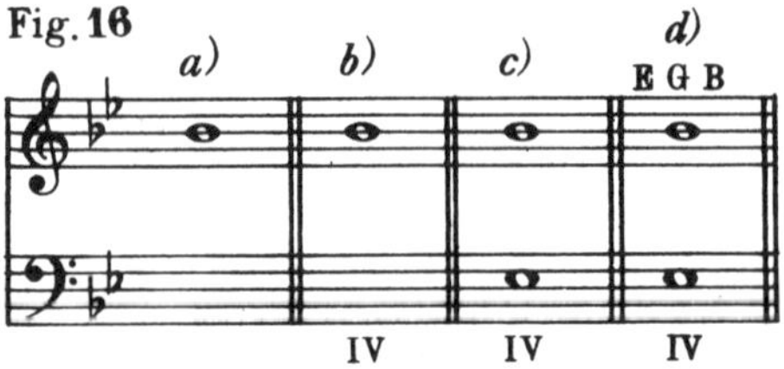

a)   b)   c)   d)

E G B

IV   IV   IV

(1) Decide to which chord or chords it belongs. (See Chapter I, para. 9.) B♭ is doh. Doh belongs to I and IV, so either chord can be chosen. We will choose IV Write this numeral under the bass. Fig. 16 (*b*).

(2) Write in the bass note. Fig. 16 (c).

(3) Write the names of the notes required above the treble staff. Fig. 16 (*d*). Remember to think *upwards* from the bass.

Now continue as in para. 9 (4)–(9).

**Exercise II.** Add parts for A.T.B. to each melody note given in Fig. 17. Give two arrangements where possible.

**Fig. 17**

a)   b)   c)   d)   e)        f)   g)   h)   i)   j)

SUMMARY OF RULES GIVEN IN THIS CHAPTER.

(1) Vocal range. Keep within the limits shown in Fig. 1.

(2) Generally double the root. It is possible to double the 5th. Do not double the 3rd.

(3) The 5th may be omitted, but not the 3rd.

(4) Do not have the tenor too low down, particularly if it is a 3rd from the bass.

(5) Do not have more than an octave between adjacent voices, except between the bass and tenor.

(6) Do not let the parts cross.

# CHAPTER IV.

## MELODIC PROGRESSION

(Part I, Chapter II, Intervals, should have been worked before studying this chapter.)

1 MELODIC PROGRESSION. The movement from note to note in any one part is called " melodic progression "

2 UNACCOMPANIED MELODY. When a melody is sung or played by itself it needs to have plenty of movement and variety. It can move freely, as it is unfettered by the movement of other parts. *e.g.* :—

**Fig. 1**

POP GOES THE WEASEL

3 MELODY IN COUNTERPOINT. When two or more melodies are combined the result forms a texture which we term " counterpoint " (the adjective is " contrapuntal "). *e.g.* :—

**Fig. 2**

PRELUDE 14 OF THE "48"                                    *Bach*

It is very difficult to combine melodies in such a way that they are interesting in themselves and yet sound well together, so we shall not attempt this at present.

4 MELODY IN SIMPLE HARMONY. When several parts are moving together, as in simple four part harmony, each part moves in a much more smooth and simple fashion. Notice how smoothly the parts move in Fig. 3, and how many repeated notes there are, particularly in alto and tenor.

**Fig. 3**
Hymn Tune (STUTTGART)

This kind of writing is easier to sing, write, and listen to, so we shall learn to do this first.

5 MELODY IN COMPOSITION. The best kind of composition (apart from very simple pieces) though written in harmony, frequently has parts moving contrapuntally, and interesting " counter melodies " moving at the same time as the main melody. Fig. 4 shows Wagner, in a particularly fine example, combining three tunes at once, (*a*) the Prize Song, (*b*) a March, (*c*) the theme of the Mastersingers, and having supporting harmonies at the same time !

**Fig. 4**

MASTERSINGERS OVERTURE

*Wagner*

The more advanced your study becomes, the more do harmony and counterpoint merge into one, and become composition. But it is easier to study them separately at first.

6 SMOOTHNESS. The smoother a vocal part the easier it is to sing. The whole effect will not sound too dull, as the chords are constantly changing. When parts begin to move about more freely the harmonies change less frequently.

Your bass part cannot be smooth at present, as you can use only doh, fah and soh. But the other parts should either stay on the same note (binding note), or move a 2nd or 3rd most of the time. At present, if an inner part moves

more than a 4th you can suspect there is something wrong !
There will probably be an alternative which will produce
smoother movement between the chords. Look again at
Fig. 3.

7 CONJUNCT AND DISJUNCT MOVEMENT. When a part
moves by step it is said to proceed in " conjunct " movement. When it moves by leap (even if the leap is only a 3rd),
disjunct movement is produced.

8 USE OF LEAPS. Occasionally you will find the bass, or
even the treble, leaping an octave. In such a case be careful
that the notes before and after the leap are inside the octave,
as in Fig. 5 and Fig. 6 (*a*). How would you like to sing
Fig. 6 (*b*) ?

**Fig. 5**

CHRISTIANS AWAKE (STOCKPORT)

Fig. **6**

ANNIE LAURIE

Octaves are more common than 6ths and 7ths, which are
awkward to sing and had better be avoided at present, particularly in inner parts. The 6th may occasionally be used
in an outside part if you are sure it sounds well. After any
big leap it is advisable to let the next note be inside it, as at
† in Fig. 7. Leaps are generally good if they occur between
two positions of the same chord.

Try to sing Fig. 7 at sight. (It is, of course, much
easier if you have heard it played first, so it would then be

no fair test.) *You* may be able to sing it, but the average member of a school or church choir could not.

9 MENTAL EFFECTS. The mental effects of the notes of the scale have been spoken of in Part I, Chapter I. You should always be conscious of them. You know, *e.g.*, that fah often goes to me, and te usually goes to doh.

10 TE. Sing the soprano of the examples in Fig. 8 while the chords are played, and decide which tes move naturally to the next note and which sound wrong.

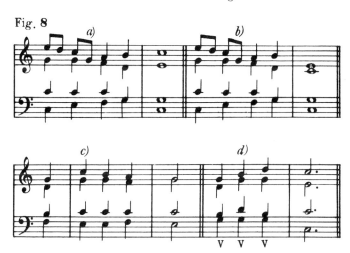

You will probably decide that (*a*), (*c*) and (*d*) sound satisfactory and (*b*) sounds wrong—because doh is expected. From your previous knowledge and from these examples you can frame the following rules :—

1 Te almost always rises, and usually goes to doh.
  It should always move to doh at a cadence.

Bach frequently moves te down to soh in an alto part at a cadence, in order to have a complete tonic chord. See Fig. 9. But at this stage it is not advisable for you to do so.

**Fig. 9**

(2) Te can occasionally move to lah when a part is moving doh te lah.

(3) When V is repeated te can move to another note of the same chord, but te in the last V must move to doh.

11 DIMINISHED AND AUGMENTED INTERVALS. In Part I, Chapter II, you discovered that diminished and augmented intervals were discords, and that there was one augmented interval, fah to te, and one diminished interval, te to fah, in a major key.

You will not be able to use te and fah in the same chord (*i.e.*, harmonically) until Part III, as the Primary Triads do not contain these notes in any one chord. But they may occur melodically. Sight sing Fig. 10 and make comments.

Fig. **10**

(*a*) is awkward, and cannot be successfully sung by average singers ; (*b*) and (*d*) are quite satisfactory ; (*c*) and (*e*) sound wrong.

So these rules can be formulated :—

(1) Do not use augmented intervals melodically at all.

(2) Only use a diminished interval melodically if the next note moves inside it.

**Exercise I.** Your understanding and knowledge of this chapter will be shown when you come to work exercises in Chapter V. In the meantime you can sing the fragments of melody in Fig. 11 to sol-fa, and make comments on their suitability for use in a hymn tune or a simple song.

Fig. **11**

SUMMARY OF RULES.

(1) Move smoothly, not often more than a 3rd in the inside parts.

(2) When there is a leap of more than a 4th the next note should be inside the leap.

7

(3) 8ves are better than 6ths and 7ths in a melodic part.

(4) Te should almost always rise, and usually to doh. Exceptions :—

    (*a*) It can move to lah, when a part is moving doh, te, lah.

    (*b*) It can move to another note when V is repeated, but the last te must rise to doh.

Te should always rise to doh at a cadence.

(5) Do not use an augmented interval—(fah te, major key).

(6) If a diminished interval is used, the next note must be inside it.

## CHAPTER V.

### HARMONIC PROGRESSION

**1** HARMONIC PROGRESSION. When two or more parts move together the movement is called " harmonic progression ". In the course of time musicians have discovered that some harmonic progressions sound better than others, so that nowadays we can make rules, based on the work of the great composers. It is wise to follow their footsteps to begin with, until your ear becomes more perceptive. When you have " grown up " musically, and have developed artistic judgment, there will be nothing to prevent your breaking all the rules if you wish ! You will break them more artistically if you understand the reason for them. That is quite different from breaking them because your ear is faulty and you know no better.

The rules are based on music of the past. Mozart and Beethoven do not make such bad models! The next generation will have to formulate the rules and principles of the advanced music of to-day. But the changes in music that have come to stay, like those in all the arts, have always grown out of the past—" evolution ", and not " revolution ".

**2** OVERLAPPING. Look at Fig. 1 (*a*). You will see that the bass goes higher in the second chord than the tenor was in the first. Similarly in (*b*) the soprano goes lower in the second chord than the alto was in the first. This effect is called " overlapping ". The encroaching of one part on another in this way is better avoided.

**Fig. 1**

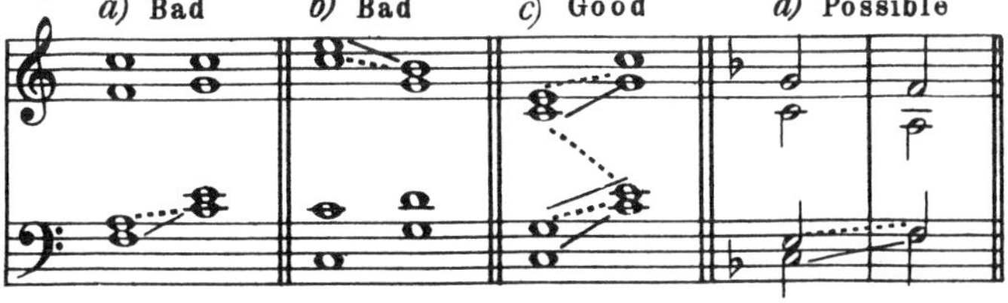

*a)* Bad    *b)* Bad    *c)* Good    *d)* Possible

Overlapping is, however, satisfactory between two positions of the same chord, as at (*c*). Sing (*a*), (*b*) and (*c*) if possible, so as to hear the effects. It is also occasionally written at a perfect cadence, when te doh is in the tenor, to avoid too low a bass note. Cf. (*d*) and (*e*).

When one part sings a note that the other has just left, as in Fig. 1 ( *f* ), it is not overlapping, and it is quite correct.

3 DIFFERENT KINDS OF MOTION. There are three possible kinds of motion between any two melodic parts :—

(*a*) *Oblique motion.* One part stays while the other part moves. Fig. 2 (*a*).

(*b*) *Similar motion.* The parts move in the same direction. Fig. 2 (*b*) and (*c*). It is parallel as well as similar motion, if they move the same distance, as at (*b*).

(*c*) *Contrary motion.* The parts move in opposite directions. Fig. 2 (*d*).

**Fig. 2**

**Exercise I.** Name the kind of motion used between all the parts in Fig. 3. Six intervals are being made in each chord, viz. : S. and A. ; S. and T. ; S. and B. ; A. and T. ; A. and B. ; T. and B., so there are six sets of movement to name. Work thus :—

S.+A. chords 1—2 oblique ;   2—3 contrary, etc.
S.+T. chords 1—2 similar ;   2—3 oblique,  etc.

**Fig. 3**

**Exercise II.** Work through Fig. 3 again, naming the intervals made between the parts, thus :—

S.+A., 1, 3, 6, etc.

S.+T., 6, 6, 8, etc.

4 CONSECUTIVE INTERVALS. If two parts move in similar parallel motion, they will obviously repeat the interval they make. So now let us decide which repeated intervals will sound well. Sing all the intervals in Fig. 4, and see if you agree with the following comments :—

**Fig. 4**

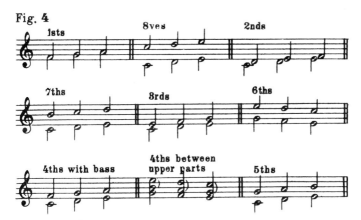

*Consecutive 1sts and 8ves.* These are satisfactory. But if the singing is supposed to be in four *different* parts, it will sound like a mistake if two parts do the same thing for a few notes. (Have you noticed how thin and queer it sounds if a part gets lost in a singing class, and merges into another part by mistake ?)  Of course, it is satisfactory if it is done for at least a whole phrase.  Some hymns do this occasionally. *e.g.*, Fig. 5.

**Fig. 5**

WE PLOUGH THE FIELDS

Other hymns drop some of their voice parts for a short time, as it is effective to bring them in again, one by one. *e.g.*, Fig. 6.

*Fig.* **6**

O COME, ALL YE FAITHFUL

But in a short exercise of the kind you write, it is better to keep to four part harmony throughout, and write no consecutive 1sts and 8ves.

If the bass has consecutive octaves with a part which is not immediately above it, it not only sounds thin, but crude.

Compare Fig. 7 (*a*) with (*b*). It is, of course, very common to double the bass in octaves as at (*c*), particularly in piano writing, but it is not sensible in writing for four different voice parts. Similarly a melody is often strengthened by doubling at the 8ve. See (*d*).

**Fig. 7**

Beethoven Op. 10. No 1

*Consecutive 2nds and 7ths.* These are ugly. However, as no chord containing a 2nd or a 7th will be considered until Part IV, you can forget about them for the time being.

*Consecutive 3rds and 6ths.* These are very good. In two part writing it would be dull to have consecutive 3rds or 6ths for long, but in four part harmony other parts are making variety, so you can write as many as you like. See Fig. 8.

**Fig. 8**

*Consecutive 4ths.* 4ths with the bass are discordant. However, you cannot write them until you learn about 2nd inversions, so this also you can forget about. 4ths between upper parts are good.

*Consecutive 5ths.* A 5th by itself sounds bare, and when two are consecutive they sound crude. Try to hear all the 5ths in Fig. 9. They sound much worse between the outside parts. Compare the effect with that of Fig. 8.

**Fig. 9**

5ths occasionally sound effective when used for a special purpose, and when complicated discords are used they cannot always be heard. But they will always sound crude to a discerning ear, in the kind of harmony you write at present, even if *your* ear is not good enough to dislike them !

Pupils frequently make up two new rules for themselves at this stage, so you shall be forewarned :—

(1) A 1st, 5th or 8ve repeated at the same pitch is satisfactory because there is no *movement.*

(2) A 5th moving to a 1st or 8ve or *vice versa* is satisfactory because there are no *consecutives*.

But a 1st moving to an 8ve, or *vice versa*, is not good, as in spite of the contrary movement, the two parts are singing the same notes.

To sum up, consecutive 3rds and 6ths, and 4ths between upper parts, are good, but not consecutive 1sts, 5ths and 8ves. Other consecutive intervals are not possible until your harmonic vocabulary is extended.

5 KIND OF MOTION TO USE.

*Oblique motion.* Use plenty of oblique motion, as it involves the use of binding notes and smooth parts. But do not use a binding note in one part if it means that another part has a big leap. Consider the smoothness of *both* parts.

*Similar motion.* This is satisfactory when the movement is not parallel and there are therefore no consecutive intervals. When the movement is parallel, consecutive 3rds and 6ths and consecutive 4ths between upper parts can be used. But be on your guard against parallel motion, as it may produce the forbidden consecutive 1sts, 5ths or 8ves.

*Contrary motion.* Use as much of this as possible, particularly between the bass and the upper parts. The movement of parts can be heard better when they are moving away from each other, and it is almost impossible to produce the forbidden consecutives. You *might* get 5ths or 8ves as in Fig. 10 (*a*) and (*b*), but you have no right to be moving as much as a 5th in an inner part ! There is sure to be a smoother way. Rearrange the examples yourselves. However, consecutive 5ths and 8ves do not sound as bad in contrary as in similar motion.

Fig. 10

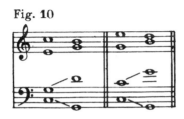

6 LOOKING FOR FORBIDDEN CONSECUTIVES. Try to hear faulty consecutives. But if your ear is not very good you may not always do so. It is the best way of detecting them, so continue to train your ear ; in the meantime you can always see them.

The quickest method is to correct a chord immediately it is written, and only look carefully at those parts which are moving in parallel, similar motion (*i.e.*, the only parts which can make forbidden consecutives).

Fig. 11

Look at the examples in Fig. 11 :—

(*a*) You can see at a glance that S. and A. move down by step, T. is a binding note, and B. leaps down. . ˙ . T. and B. can cause no trouble ; only S. and A. need their intervals naming. Are they satisfactory ?

(*b*) S. moves down, A. moves up by step, T. and B. leap up. Only T. and B. need their intervals naming. Are they satisfactory ?

(*c*) S. is a binding note, A., T. and B. leap up. A. + T., A. + B., and T. + B. need correcting. Are they satisfactory ?

(*d*) S., A., T. and B. all move up by step. Now there are plenty of intervals to correct, all the six sets, in fact ! Are they satisfactory ?

You will rarely find more than one set of parts to correct, and if you follow the directions given in this chapter you should find no faults. In harmony, one fault has a nasty habit of producing others ! It pays to work carefully and intelligently from the beginning, and it saves time too.

**Exercise III.** Name all the forbidden consecutives in Fig. 12. Then sing it through to hear the effect.

Fig. **12**

7 ROOTS RISING OR FALLING A 2ND. When using IV V, or V IV the smoothest progression is obtained by letting every part move by step in similar motion. But you see the trouble this caused in Fig. 11 (*d*). There will be a 5th and a doubled root somewhere, so obviously consecutive 5ths and 8ves will occur. The trouble will always arise when roots rise or fall a 2nd. So always move contrary with the 5th and 8ve from the bass, in such a case. You are not bound to move contrary with the 3rd, but generally it is easier to let *all* the parts move contrary to the bass. See Fig. 13.

Fig. **13**

8 5TH OMITTED FROM CHORD. Occasionally it may happen that the 5th has to be left out of a chord and the root used three times, in order to avoid a faulty progression. This is bound to happen in Fig. 14 (*a*) and (*b*) if melody and bass are given. Try other arrangements for yourself without altering the melody and bass, and see what faults appear.

**Fig. 14**

9 HOW TO WORK AN EXERCISE WHEN MELODY AND BASS
ARE GIVEN. Both melody and bass are given at this stage,
so that you can give full attention to harmonic movement.

The following method of working is musical and accurate.
It will become quick and automatic after a time, and some
stages can then be left out.

PRELIMINARIES.

(1) Name the key.

(2) Sing the melody to sol-fa.

(3) Sing the bass to sol-fa.

(4) Try to hear both together. Then check your hearing
by playing.

(5) Write the Roman numerals under the bass.

(6) Put a X under the bass stave where the bass moves
by step, as a warning to move contrary with the 5th
and 8ve from the bass.

(7) Write " te " above the treble stave over every V, to
remind yourself it requires consideration.

FILLING IN.

(1) Name the notes which belong to the first chord, and
write them over the chord. Cross out the ones you
already have.

(2) Decide which notes to use for alto and tenor, and
place them.

(3) Write the second chord in the same way. Use :—

    (*a*) Binding notes where possible.

    (*b*) Smooth movement, rarely more than a 3rd.

    (*c*) Contrary motion to the bass where there is a X.

    (*d*) Te correctly.

CHECKING. As soon as each chord is written check immediately :—

(1) *Each separate chord.* Try to hear each chord separately, and check for (*a*) correct notes, doubling and omitting ; (*b*) correct spacing and range, and no crossing.

(2) *Melodic movement.* Sing the melody of each part you have added (*i.e.*, alto and tenor) to sol-fa. Check for (*a*) smooth movement ; (*b*) te moving correctly ; (*c*) no augmented intervals (fah te, major key) ; (*d*) diminished intervals moving inwards (te fah, major key).

(3) *Harmonic movement.* Try to hear the harmonic movement from one chord to the next. Check for (1) no overlapping ; (2) no consecutive 1sts, 5ths or 8ves. (Look for them as shown in para. 6.)

*Continuation.* Continue with the next chord in the same way. If you find it impossible to move correctly at a given point it may be necessary to begin again with the alto and tenor changed round. A low tenor often makes difficulties. When you have come to the end try to hear the final result. Then sing the exercise in parts if you are in class. If you are alone try it through on the piano.

**Exercise IV.** Add alto and tenor to the following exercises, working as shown in para. 9. Work with the book open, until you know the procedure from memory. [All exercises in ⁶⁄₈ time in Parts II and III of this book are in slow ⁶⁄₈ (6 beats) and not quick ⁶⁄₈ (2 beats).]

Fig. 15

EAR TESTS. The teacher should play the primary triads in various arrangements, two or three chords at a time. The pupil can be asked to (*a*) name the chords, (*b*) name the chords and melody notes, or (*c*) write the outside parts in notation, at the discretion of the teacher. Fig. 16 shows a few specimen tests.

Fig. 16

SUMMARY OF RULES AND CHORD PROGRESSIONS.

(1) Do not overlap, except (*a*) between two positions of the same chord, (*b*) between tenor and bass at a perfect cadence, when the tenor sings te doh.

(2) Do not write consecutive 1sts, 5ths or 8ves.

(3) In using IV and V together the 5th and 8ve must move in contrary motion to the bass.

# CHAPTER VI.

## HARMONISING A MELODY

1 HARMONISING A MELODY. We now come to a much more interesting stage, as, for the first time, you are to choose your own chords for harmonising a melody. When both outside parts are given, harmony is little more than a kind of arithmetic. Now you will have to exercise your ear and your musical judgment, to get an artistic result.

2 POSSIBLE CHORD CHOICE WITH I, IV AND V. As you know only three chords however, your choice will be very limited at present. Revise Part II, Chapter I, para. 9. Only two melody notes, doh and soh, can have a choice of chord. Your choice is further limited by the conditions stated in paras. 3–7 of this chapter.

3 ACCENT AND CHORD CHOICE. With the freshness of a new strong accent comes the desire for the freshness of a new chord. Play Fig. 1 (a) and (b) up to speed. Can you feel the halting effect at * in (b), even though the melody note is changed on the accent ? Compare it with † in (b) where, because the chord is changed, the sound is satisfactory, in spite of the repeated melody note.

**Fig.1**

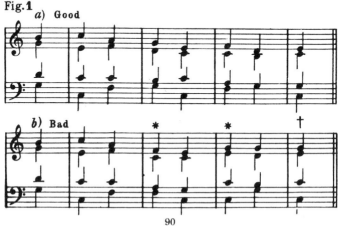

If you do not dislike the effect at *, blame your inexperienced ear once more ! Musicians are more conscious of this than of many other faults.

Remember that, in four time, the third beat of the bar has an accent as well as the first, and that in slow ⁶⁄₈ time there are also two accents in each bar.

In hymn tunes the same chord is sometimes used ‿—for the first two notes. *e.g.*, Fig. 2.

**Fig. 2** HANOVER

This is the only exception you must allow yourself. It is generally good to use the same chord —‿, and such progressions are very frequent. Play Fig. 3 as written. Then play it with all the bar lines a beat forward, and hear how awkward it sounds.

**Fig. 3**

It is better to change the chord on the third beat than on the second, in three time, if you have the choice. Your chord rhythm is then ♩ ♩, instead of ♩ ♩, which tends to sound syncopated. Fig. 4 (*a*) is better than (*b*).

8

4 ANTICIPATING THE CADENCE. Do not use the final cadence chord on the previous strong accent, even if it has a different melody note. It spoils the effect of the cadence. Cf. Fig. 5 (*a*) and (*b*).

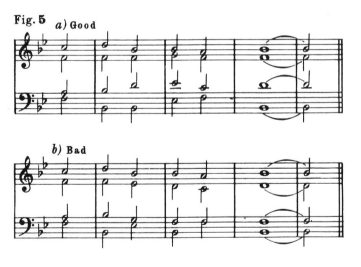

5 HARMONISING DOH ON AN ACCENT. Avoid harmonising doh with I on an accent, except for the final chord or (occasionally) on the first strong accent. It sounds too final.

6 V IV.  Avoid V IV, as it does not generally sound well.
Play Fig. 6 (*a*) and (*b*) and then change round the second
and third chords in both examples, so that V IV becomes
IV V, and hear how much better the examples sound. V
IV sounds best when the melody moves ray fah, as in Fig.
6 (*c*).

**Fig. 6**

Any other combination of chords you can use at present
will sound well.

7 EXPOSED 5THS AND 8VES IN OUTSIDE PARTS.  When the
*outside* parts move by *similar* motion to a 5th or 8ve there
is danger that the 5th or 8ve will stand out unexpectedly
and sound wrong.  Play Fig. 7 (*a*) and (*b*).  (*a*) sounds
awkward ; at (*b*) the same chord is approached by contrary
motion and sounds quite satisfactory.  Similarly compare
the approach to the 8ve in (*c*) and (*d*).

These " exposed " 5ths and 8ves do not stand out if the melody moves by step. *E.g.*, Fig. 8 (*a*) and (*b*). But where possible, it is better to move in contrary motion. Fig. 8 (*c*) is slightly better than (*a*). Exposed 5ths and 8ves do not sound wrong between two positions of the same chord, as at (*d*).

Do not make things impossible by trying to apply this rule to *all* the parts ! The intervals are only " exposed " in the outside parts.

8 MELODIC LINE OF BASS. Your bass is bound to be ungainly at present. But frequently you have the choice of moving to the top or bottom octave for a note. Move to the octave which makes the smoothest line, keeps within the bass range, and avoids exposed 5ths and 8ves. Fig. 9 (*a*) is a better bass line than (*b*), which is too jumpy, and too low in one place.

**Fig. 9**

Sometimes you will find yourself in difficulties because the bass is getting in the way of the tenor. If it is your own bass there is nothing to prevent your changing it. You may find that the whole or part of it can go an 8ve lower, and your difficulty is solved without changing any upper parts. Cf. Fig. 9 (*a*) and (*c*).

9 HOW TO HARMONISE CADENCES. This is only a little more difficult than the work of the previous chapter. As you know what chords can be used at a cadence, you know what the bass must be. *e.g.* : You are to harmonise the melody of Fig. 10 (*a*). Ray belongs to V, me belongs to I, so there is no choice. Write in your bass as at (*b*), and continue as shown in the last chapter.

**Fig. 10**

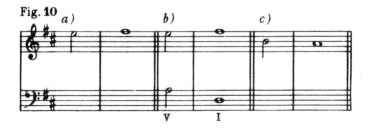

Now harmonise Fig. 10 (*c*). Lah belongs to IV, soh to V and I. If you choose V you write an imperfect cadence ; if I, a plagal cadence. Fill in the bass of your choice and **continue as before.**

**Exercise 1.** Harmonise the following cadences :—

10 HOW TO HARMONISE A MELODY.  Work as follows :—

(1) Name the key.

(2) Sing the melody to sol-fa.

(3) Decide what cadence the last two melody notes make, and write the Roman numerals under the bass stave.

(4) Starting at the beginning, write Roman numerals under the rest of the bass notes. Where there is a choice of chord write both.

(5) Write in the bass—both notes where there is a choice.

(6) Decide which bass note to choose, where there is a preference, and rub the other one out. (Refer to paras. 3–7 if necessary.)

(7) Sing the bass to sol-fa. Check for (*a*) false accent ; (*b*) anticipating the cadence ; (*c*) melodic line.

(8) Try to hear the melody and bass together. Check for (*a*) using I on an accent when doh is at the top, except for the final chord, or (occasionally) on the first strong accent ; (*b*) use of IV V and V IV ; (*c*) exposed 5ths and 8ves ; (*d*) consecutive 5ths and 8ves. (Name the intervals throughout.)

(9) Put a X under the bass stave where the bass moves by step, and write te above the treble stave wherever V is used.

Then fill in and check as shown in Chapter V, para. 9.

**Exercise II.** Harmonise the following melodies. Follow the plan described above. When you have formed good habits, you may feel that some stages can safely be left out. In time, you will be able to tell at a glance that a progression " looks " right, without detailed checking.

Fig. 12

EAR TESTS. No new type is required in this or the next chapter. But some tests should be given every week, either in the aural training or the harmony lesson, or both.

SUMMARY OF RULES AND CHORD PROGRESSIONS.

(1) The same chord should not be used ∪—. It is good —∪.

(2) The final cadence chord should not be used on the previous strong accent.

(3) Avoid harmonising doh with I on an accent except for the final chord, or (occasionally) on the first strong accent.

(4) Avoid using V IV, unless the melody is ray fah.

(5) Avoid exposed 5ths and 8ves (outside parts) unless (*a*) the top part moves by step ; (*b*) between two positions of the same chord.

## CHAPTER VII.

## HARMONISING A BASS

1 HARMONISING A BASS. When you harmonise a bass, at present, the chords are chosen for you, as the bass note must be the root of the chord. But when you have learnt inversions you will find that sometimes a bass note can have a choice of chord, which is more interesting.

2 POSSIBLE MELODY NOTES. There is, however, much more choice of melody than there was choice of bass when the melody was given. Each bass note may have a 3rd or 5th or 8ve above it. Use the 3rd as much as possible, particularly on an accent, as it is softer than the 5th or 8ve.

3 MELODIC LINE OF SOPRANO. Move smoothly, generally to the nearest note, but try not to run too much round the same notes. Such " tautology " is more noticeable in the melody than in the inner parts. Get a good melodic curve, with a climax if possible.

Avoid doh as the melody note over I on a strong accent, except for the final chord and (occasionally) the first strong accent.

4 RULES. There are no new rules, but you are reminded of the following three, as they affect your choice of melody note :—

(a) Move contrary with the 5th and 8ve from the bass, when using IV and V together.

(b) Avoid consecutive 5ths and 8ves.

(c) Avoid exposed 5ths and 8ves.

5 EXAMPLES. Fig. 1 shows three different melodies added to the same bass. (a) is good, (b) and (c) are poor. Play all three. Then name the faults and weaknesses in (b) and (c).

**Fig. 1**

6 HOW TO HARMONISE A CADENCE.  Work as follows :—

(1) Put the Roman numerals under the bass.

(2) Choose the melody notes.

(3) Fill in, as shown in Chapter V.

**Exercise I.**  Harmonise the following cadences :—

**Fig. 2**

7 HOW TO HARMONISE A BASS.   Work as follows :—

(1) Name the key.

(2) Sing the bass to sol-fa.

(3) Write the Roman numerals under the bass.

(4) Put a X under the bass where IV V or V IV is used, and te over the treble where V is used.

(5) Add a melody, checking each note as you write it (refer to paras. 2–4 if necessary).

(6) Sing the melody to sol-fa and check it.

(7) Try to hear the melody and bass together. Check for (*a*) avoidance of doh over I on a strong accent, except for the final chord or (occasionally) on the first strong accent ; (*b*) use of IV V, and V IV ; (*c*) exposed 5ths and 8ves ; (*d*) consecutive 5ths and 8ves. (Name the intervals throughout.)

Then fill in and check as shown in Chapter V, para. 9.

**Exercise II.** Harmonise the following basses.. Keep the book open until you know the order of working from memory.

Fig. **3**

SUMMARY OF RULES AND CHORD PROGRESSIONS.

(1) Use plenty of 3rds from the bass in the melody (particularly on the accents) as they are a little softer than 5ths and 8ves.

(2) Move smoothly in the melody, but not too much round the same notes. Get a good melodic curve with a climax, if possible.

(3) Avoid doh as the melody note over I on a strong accent except for the final chord or (occasionally) on the first strong accent.

# CHAPTER VIII.

## I, IV, V MINOR KEY.  PIANO ARRANGEMENT

(Only the harmonic form of the minor scale needs to be known before studying this chapter.)

1 SCOPE OF THE NEXT TWO CHAPTERS.  The next two chapters cover the ground of the previous chapters in Part II, but with reference to the minor key.  Therefore, in addition to giving practice in the minor key, they also provide a most useful means of revision.  Work should gradually become much quicker.  But it should still be done in a methodical way ;  it does not save time to work in a haphazard fashion.

2 I, IV, V MINOR KEY.  Play the scale of C (harmonic) minor and then pick out the notes of I, IV, V from it.  You get Fig. 1*b*.

**Fig. 1**

Sing the scale of C major, then Fig. 1 (*a*) in parts.  Then sing the scale of C minor and Fig. 1 (*b*) in parts.  Compare Fig. 1 (*a*) and (*b*) and you will discover the following :—

| *Major Key.* | *Minor Key.* |
|---|---|
| I   Major triad d,m,s | Minor triad d, *maw*, s |
| IV Major triad f,l,d | Minor triad f, *law*, d |
| V  Major triad s,t,r | Major triad s, t, r. |

3 DIFFERENCES OF SOUND, MAJOR AND MINOR KEY.  I and IV have a flattened third in the minor key, as compared with the tonic major.  V sounds the same in major and minor key, being a major triad in both keys.

You can easily recognise V in a minor key because it is the only major triad you know.

Play Fig. 15, Part II, Chapter II (Auld Lang Syne harmonised with primary triads) and then compare it with the sound of Fig. 2 below, a minor tune harmonised with primary triads. Then play Auld Lang Syne in the minor and the Jolly Miller in the major, in order to hear the difference.

**Fig. 2** THE JOLLY MILLER

EAR TESTS. Recognition of the difference between major and minor triads has been practised in Part I, Chapter III. So the teacher can now go straight on to the recognition of I, IV and V in the minor key. After the key has been established, triads should be played as in Fig. 1 (*b*). The pupil should use sol-fa.

**Exercise I.** Play the primary triads in a major key, as in Fig. 1 (*a*). Then play them in the tonic minor, as in Fig. 1 (*b*), by changing me to maw in I, and lah to law in IV. V remains unchanged. Do this with a number of keys.

4 DIFFERENCES OF NOTATION, MAJOR AND MINOR KEY. You have been told how to find the key signature of a minor key in Part I, Chapter IV.

Look again at Fig. 1 in this chapter. Notice that the aural effect and the notation seem to contradict one another.

Apart from the key signature, I and IV look alike in major and minor key, though they sound different. We can never tell, by looking at the position of notes on the staff, whether chords are major or minor. But V, which sounds just the same in major and minor key, looks different, as in the minor key, though still diatonic, it requires an accidental. There is a danger of forgetting this, because we do not hear a chromatic sound. So be on your guard !

**Exercise II.** Write the primary triads in various minor keys as in Fig. 1. Remember te !

5 THREE NOTES IN CLOSE POSITION. Fig. 3 shows I, IV, V in C minor arranged in close position for the piano :—

Fig. 3

Arranged for equal voices for singing :—

Fig. 4

Notice that the accidental must be written again if the same note is sung by a different voice.

EAR TESTS. The teacher should give the following kinds of ear tests :—

(*a*) Minor triads without relation to a key, the pupil to say whether the root, 3rd, or 5th is at the top. He must find out whether the top note sounds like doh, maw, or soh. *e.g.*, Fig. 5.

**Fig. 5**

(*b*) I, IV, V played in isolation after the key has been established, the pupil to say which chord is being played. *e.g.*, Fig. 6.

**Fig. 6**

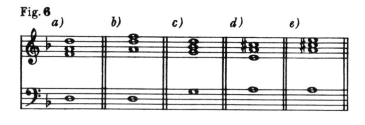

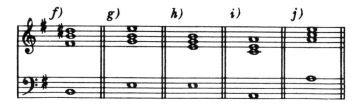

(*c*) I, IV, V played as in Fig. 6, the pupil to say which note is at the top, in addition to naming the chord.

**Exercise III.** Play I, IV, V in the three close positions in various minor keys, as isolated chords. There are no new directions, but refer to Part II, Chapter I, para. 7, if necessary.

**Exercise IV.** Write I, IV, V in the three close positions in various minor keys, as isolated chords.

6 JOINING TRIADS WITH BINDING NOTES. The binding notes between I and V, and I and IV are the same in major and minor keys. *e.g.* :—

**Fig. 7**

Arranged for equal voices for singing :—

**Fig. 8**

**Exercise V.** Play (*a*) I V, (*b*) I IV, (*c*) V I, (*d*) IV I in various minor keys, three notes in the right hand and one in the left. Keep a binding note. Refer to Part II, Chapter II, para. 2, if necessary.

**Exercise VI.** As Exercise V, but write the progressions.

EAR TESTS. The teacher should play similar progressions for the pupil to recognise. (Examples given in Fig. 5, Chapter II, might be played in the minor key.)

7 CADENCES. The presence or absence of the major chord V should help in the recognition of cadences. Turn to Fig. 6 in Part II, Chapter II. Play each example as written first, then imagine the key signature of C minor, and B♮ where it is required, and play in the minor key. Treat Figs. 7 to 12 similarly, playing or singing as required. Use sol-fa when singing.

(*Note.*—The tune in Figs. 6 and 8 requires altering as in Fig. 9 below. This may be a good moment for showing the need for the melodic form of the minor scale).

9

Fig. **9**

Alteration of Tunes
*a)* Fig. 6 Part II. Ch. II.

8 PICARDY THIRD. You will sometimes find that the last chord of a piece in the minor key has a major 3rd. This is called a *tierce de picardie* or Picardy 3rd. It does not change the key, but is merely a chromatic note in the minor key. Bach, when writing in a minor key, more often ends with a major than a minor 3rd. *E.g.*, Fig. 10. Use a Picardy 3rd at a cadence whenever you wish.

Fig. **10** END OF FUGUE N? 2 OF "THE 48" *Bach*

EAR TESTS. The teacher should give similar tests to those quoted in Part II, Chapter II, Fig. 13.

**Exercise VII.** Play perfect, imperfect and plagal cadences in various major and minor keys, three notes in the right hand in close position and one in the left. Keep a binding note. I V is the only imperfect cadence you should play.

**Exercise VIII.** As Exercise VII, but write the cadences.

# CHAPTER IX.

## I, IV, V MINOR KEY ; VOICE PARTS

1 WRITING FOR VOICE PARTS. ISOLATED CHORDS. There is nothing new under this heading. But remember that te requires an accidental.

**Exercise I.** Add S., A. and T. to the following bass notes. Give three arrangements of each.

**Fig.1**

**Exercise II.** Add A.T.B. to the following melody notes. Give two arrangements where possible.

**Fig. 2**

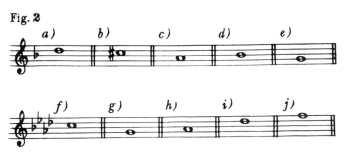

2 HARMONIC AND MELODIC MINOR. Part I, Chapter IV, describes two forms of the minor scale, harmonic and melodic, and states why the harmonic form is the foundation of harmony in the minor key, in spite of the fact that it causes difficulties with regard to augmented intervals. Later you will be shown how to avoid some of these by the use of the melodic minor, but for the present we shall keep to the harmonic form.

3 MELODIC PROGRESSION IN THE MINOR KEY. You know that there are four augmented intervals : (1) maw te, (2) fah te (as in the major), (3) law te and (4) law ray. Three of these are concerned with te, which you are watching in any case. Notice that soh is the only note which can rise to te : see Fig. 3 (*a*). If te is approached from above as at Fig. 3 (*b*), then the augmented intervals become diminished, and all is well, provided that the next note is inside the leap.

**Fig. 3**

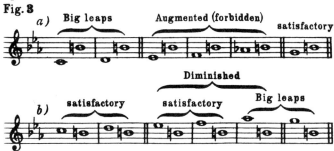

If you always sing melodic parts to sol-fa you should quickly be conscious of augmented and diminished intervals. They are particularly likely to occur in using IV V and V IV.

**Exercise III.** Make comments on the following melodic parts :—

**Fig. 4**

**4** HARMONIC PROGRESSION IN THE MINOR KEY. In using IV V and V IV major key, contrary motion to the bass with the 5th and 8ve was used, in order to avoid consecutives, and the 3rd frequently moved in contrary motion, too. In the minor key the 3rd *must* move in contrary motion to avoid an augmented interval. Cf., Fig. 5 (*a*) and (*b*) with (*c*).

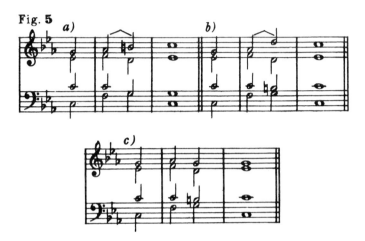

EAR TESTS. Specimen progressions are given in Fig. 6. They may be played as examples while the pupil follows in his book, or given as ear tests, at the discretion of the teacher.

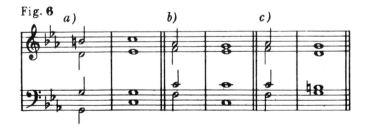

**Exercise IV.** Name all the faults in Fig. 7. There are 16 !
Analyse chord by chord.

**Exercise V.** Add alto and tenor to the following :—

**5** CADENCES. **Exercise VI.** Harmonise the following cadences :—

**Exercise VI.** Write two examples of : (*a*) a perfect cadence in G minor ; (*b*) an imperfect cadence in A minor ; (*c*) a plagal cadence in B minor.

6 RHYTHMIC VARIETY. In order to get a little rhythmic variety into the parts, you may sometimes prefer to write one long note instead of repeating a binding note, particularly in using two positions of the same chord. But be sure that the rhythm is improved by doing so ; a long note in the middle of a phrase or on a weak beat may sound wrong. Fig. 10 (*b*) is an improved version of (*a*). (*c*) is not so good ; the dotted minims in alto and bass sound halting in the middle of the phrase, also ♩ ♩ in the bass and

♩ ♩ | in the tenor sound syncopated.

**Fig. 10**

Take care that the doubling is correct at each move and that there are no faulty consecutives. Do not attempt to move more quickly than the beat.

In writing a hymn tune or chant, however, you cannot generally change repeated notes into binding notes, as there must be at least one note for every syllable of the words.

7 HARMONISING A MELODY. There is a summary of rules in the appendix and also descriptions of the method of harmonising a melody or bass. In the latter a few points are referred to which you do not yet know, but they can easily be ignored. You may prefer to use the appendix now, rather than look back into the previous chapters.

Until you are sure of the minor key, write " te = B♮ " (or whatever note it may be) above an exercise before starting to work, as a reminder of the accidental required.

**Exercise VII.** Harmonise the following melodies :—

**Fig. 11**

8 HARMONISING A BASS. When there is a long note in the bass there is no reason why the position of some or all of the upper parts should not be changed, if the result is rhythmically satisfactory, and correct. Do not move more quickly than the beat. See Fig. 12.

**Fig. 12**

Use the appendix instead of turning to previous chapters if you wish. You will realise that you cannot choose your chords as mentioned in " Method of Harmonising a Melody in Four Parts " No. 4, because at present your bass notes can only bear one chord, a root position.

**Exercise VIII.** Harmonise the following basses :—

Fig. **13**

SUMMARY OF RULES AND CHORD PROGRESSIONS.

   (1) The augmented intervals to avoid in the minor key
are : (1) maw te, (2) fah te, (3) law te, (4) law ray.

   (2) In using IV V, and V IV in the minor key, the 3rd
must move in contrary motion to the bass, as well as
the 5th and 8ve, in order to avoid augmented intervals.

   (3) Get some rhythmic variety in melodic parts by turning
repeated notes into one long note, or by moving to
another position of the same chord, where it is correct
and musical to do so. Do not move more quickly than
the beat.

## CHAPTER X.

## IB, IVB, VB, MAJOR KEY

1 REFERENCE TO PART I. Study or revise Part I, Chapter III, paras. **5** to **10**. You learn there (*a*) What a 1st inversion is ; (*b*) how it is named ; (*c*) what intervals it contains ; (*d*) how to recognise it by sound and sight ; (*e*) what I*b*, IV*b*, V*b* sound like in the major key ; and (*f*) how using occasional inversions gives a more smooth and flowing effect than can be obtained by using only root positions.

2 IMPROVED BASS LINE. The addition of I*b*, IV*b* and V*b* to your vocabulary gives six possible bass notes instead of three. So the bass can now be much more tuneful. Make a habit of noticing the bass line, which is quite as important as the soprano line. Play " Auld Lang Syne " as harmonised with root positions in Fig. 15, Part II, Chapter II, and sing the bass. Then play as shown below, again singing the bass, and hear how much more tuneful it sounds. Name all the chords, in order to see what has made the difference.

**Fig.1**

AULD LANG SYNE

3 AURAL AND VISUAL RECOGNITION. The first stage is to become familiar with the sound and look of these chords. Play Fig. 2 and listen carefully to the effect.

**Fig. 2**

Memorise the fact that me is the bass note of I*b*, lah of IV*b*, and te of V*b*. Ray is now the only note which cannot be a bass note.

EAR TESTS. The teacher should establish the key and then play I*b*, IV*b* or V*b* in isolation as in Fig. 2 (one arrangement at a time). He should tell the pupil to listen for me, lah or te in the bass and then to check by naming the melody note and seeing if it fits. Then I, IV, V should be added to the tests, so that the pupil learns to distinguish between all six chords.

**Exercise I.** Play the following progressions, listening to the effects and naming the chords :—

**Fig. 3**

4 DOUBLING AND ARRANGEMENT. Doubling is much the same as in the root position. This means that the bass note cannot generally be doubled, as it is the 3rd. The 5th is doubled rather more frequently than in the root position,

particularly when the 5th is at the top. A melody note is frequently doubled, it seems to strengthen it. Look at the doubling in all the chords in Fig. 2.

The root or the 5th may be at the top ; but the root is more common and always sounds well.

**Exercise II.** Harmonise the following bass notes, as first inversions, each in two ways. Name the root before starting, and think upwards from that.

**Exercise III.** Harmonise the following melody notes, making first inversions of primary triads in each case. Name the note to sol-fa, decide to which chord it belongs, and put the 3rd in the bass. Then fill in.

5 HARMONIC PROGRESSIONS AND DOUBLING. Only one new difficulty arises in moving from chord to chord. In IV*b* V*b* or V*b* IV*b* there is the same risk of consecutives as in IV V or V IV, and for the same reason. See Fig. 6 (*a*).

The same remedy is used, that of breaking the similar parallel motion by some contrary movement. In this case the best way is to double a different note in each chord, as at (*b*). Even the 3rd may occasionally be doubled, as at (*c*) if it moves smoothly by contrary motion to the bass, and produces a smoother part than could be obtained by doubling the 5th or 8ve. But the te in V must not be doubled, it is too sensitive, and may cause consecutive 8ves because of two tes moving to two dohs.

Notice that the use of V*b* IV*b* as at (*d*) is an instance, in the bass, of te descending by step.

Doubling is very much linked up with smoothness of melodic parts. If doubling a 5th produces a smooth part and doubling a root produces an ungainly one, then double the 5th. See the tenor part in Fig. 7 (*a*) and (*b*).

**Fig. 7**

The 3rd may also be doubled for the same reason, but only if both 3rds continue in *contrary* motion and very smoothly. Notice the doubled 3rds in Fig. 7 (*c*) and (*d*) which sound quite good. Cf. (*c*) and (*e*) which have the same second chord, but in (*e*) the doubled 3rd is not used smoothly by contrary motion. Use the doubled 3rd very sparingly, and do not double te at all, at present.

You already know that overlapping and exposed 5ths and 8ves are allowed between two positions of the same chord. An inversion counts as being the same chord, so that *e.g.*, you may write exposed 5ths between I and I*b*.

**Exercise IV.** Add alto and tenor to the following exercises. Write the Roman numerals under the bass. Think upwards from the *root*, whether it is the bass note or not.

**Fig. 8**

6 CHORD CHOICE. Having learnt *how* to use these chords, you must now learn *where* to use them. The following are some general principles :—

(*a*) Do not use the same chord ◡— even if two different positions (root and inversion) are concerned. It still sounds halting.

(*b*) Remember that 1st inversions sound well with the root at the top.

(*c*) When there is a choice remember that a 3rd or 6th between melody and bass sounds softer than a 5th or 8ve. Consecutive 3rds and 6ths or contrary motion should be used between the outside parts most of the time.

(*d*) The bass note of a 1st inversion is weaker than that of a root position and it is not good to make a big jump from it. It frequently moves by step, and rarely moves further than a 3rd. Compare the various movements of I*b* in Fig. 9. (*d*) and (*e*) might be satisfactory in some contexts, but had better be avoided for the present.

Fig. 9

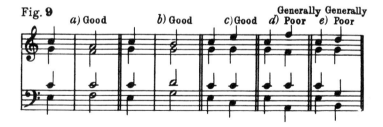

7 COMMON PROGRESSIONS. Paras. 8-10 describe the most common progressions that can be used, given I, I*b*, IV, IV*b*, V, V*b*. Notice how they carry out the principles given in para. 6.

8 TWO POSITIONS OF THE SAME CHORD. When the accent is —◡ two positions of the same chord are very good, and often preferable to a change of chord. It does not matter whether the inversion or the root position comes first. There are many possible arrangements; one of the most common is for the melody and bass to change round, while the alto and tenor remain, as at Fig. 10 (*a*). All the progressions given in Fig. 10 could be written backwards. Play them both ways.

**Fig. 10**

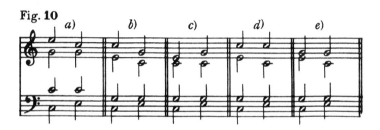

**Exercise V.** Write all the arrangements given in Fig. 10, on the chords IV IV*b* and V V*b* key C. They are just as common on these chords.

EQUAL VOICE ARRANGEMENTS. Sing Fig. 11 as written, and also sing each example backwards.

**Fig. 11**

EAR TESTS. The teacher should play two positions of the same chord, after establishing the key, and the pupil should name or write down the melody and bass.

**Exercise VI.** Harmonise the following fragments, using two positions of the same chord in each case :—

**Fig. 12**

9 FROM AN INVERSION TO A DIFFERENT ROOT POSITION. Each of the inversions you know can move to or from each root position you know, except that V*b* cannot go to IV. This is because te in the bass should either move to doh (I) ; or lah (IV*b*) descending by step ; or soh (V), another position of the same chord. If it moves to fah (IV) it creates an augmented interval (or diminished, if moving up instead of down). See Fig. 13 (*a*).

V*b* I and backwards is very common. See Fig. 13 (*b*). I*b* moves smoothly to or from IV or V, and IV*b* moves smoothly to or from V or I. See Fig. 13 (*c*) to (*h*). Play backwards also.

**Fig. 13**

Notice Fig. 13 (*b*), (*c*), (*d*) and (*e*) particularly. It is very common for the bass of a first inversion to move up a 2nd or 3rd to a root position, while the melody moves in contrary motion, and makes the intervals 6 3 with the bass. The same progressions backwards are just as good.

*Ib* IV, and *Vb* I and backwards are also common with melody and bass moving in consecutive 3rds. See Fig. 13 (*g*) and (*h*).

EQUAL VOICE ARRANGEMENTS :—

**Fig. 14**

EAR TESTS. The teacher should play progressions similar to those shown in Fig. 13 (*b*)–(*h*).

**Exercise VII.** Harmonise the following fragments, using two different chords, one of which must be inverted, in each case :—

**Fig. 15**

10 TWO FIRST INVERSIONS TOGETHER. You learnt (para. 6 (*d*)) that the bass note of a first inversion does not move very far. So the only 1st inversions it is advisable to use together at present are IV*b* and V*b*. You have already met the progressions they make in para. 5 and Fig. 6. IV*b* V*b* is more common than V*b* IV*b*. Both arrangements generally move to I for the next chord. See Fig. 16.

**Fig. 16**

EQUAL VOICE ARRANGEMENTS :—

**Fig. 17**

EAR TESTS. The teacher should play ear tests similar to the examples shown in Fig. 16.

**Exercise VIII.** Harmonise the following fragments, using IV*b* and V*b* together in each case :—

**Fig. 18**

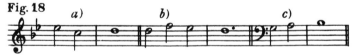

11 APPROACHES TO CADENCES. From the knowledge you have gained, make a list of all the chords that can precede V in a perfect or imperfect cadence, or IV in a plagal cadence. Put in the bar lines thus : IV*b* V | I ‖ . Remember that the final cadence chord must not be used on the previous strong accent. If it is inverted, however, it does not sound as bad. *e.g.*, I*b* V | I ‖ is possible.

Ask your teacher to play all that you have written, or write them out yourself and play them. Fig. 19 shows some good arrangements.

**Fig. 19**

12 INVERTED CADENCES. If one or both of the cadence chords are inverted, then the cadence is said to be inverted. An inverted cadence is very useful at the end of a subordinate phrase, as it does not sound too final. Play Fig. 20 (*a*) and (*b*) and hear how much more final (*a*) sounds than (*b*).

**Fig. 20**

Make a list of possible inverted cadences. Ask your teacher to play them from the list, or write them out yourself and play them. Fig. 21 shows some good arrangements. Name the cadences made.

**Fig. 21**

EAR TESTS. The teacher should play cadences similar to those shown in Figs. 19 and 21.

**Exercise IX.** Write progressions of three chords, each progression ending with the following cadences, which may be inverted if you wish : (*a*) perfect in A major ; (*b*) plagal in B♭ major ; (*c*) perfect in E major ; (*d*) imperfect in E♭ major ; (*e*) plagal in G major.

I (or I*b*) IV (a kind of imperfect cadence) is occasionally used at the end of a subordinate phrase.

13 HARMONISING THE BEGINNING OF A PHRASE. Inverted chords are often better at the beginning of a phrase also. Fig. 22 (*b*), (*c*) and (*d*) are better beginnings than (*a*), which sounds more like an ending.

**Fig. 22**

14 HARMONISING MELODIES AND BASSES. Follow the method given in the appendix. You now have more chords to choose from. Form the habit of looking for an opportunity to use common progressions, rather than thinking of one note at a time. Where there is a choice, one possibility is frequently much better than the others. Try to hear the alternatives. See what happens before and after the chord in question, and aim at contrary motion or consecutive 3rds and 6ths between the outside parts. Do not hurry over

chord choosing. It is the most important stage in the whole process, and well-chosen chords make the filling in much easier.

**Exercise X.** Harmonise the following melodies :—

**Fig. 23**

**Exercise XI.** Harmonise the following basses :—

**Fig. 24**

SUMMARY OF RULES AND CHORD PROGRESSIONS.

(1) The 5th is frequently doubled in a first inversion, particularly when it is at the top.

(2) Double the note which makes the smoothest progression. Even the 3rd may occasionally be doubled when moving smoothly in contrary motion.

(3) The root sounds well as the melody note of a first inversion ; the 5th is quite good ; the 3rd is occasionally used when moving smoothly by contrary motion.

(4) In IV*b* V*b* or V*b* IV*b*, double different notes, so as to avoid faulty consecutives.

(5) Do not use the same chord ◡—, even if one position is inverted.

(6) Outside parts should move mostly in contrary motion or consecutive 3rds and 6ths. 3rds and 6ths between melody and bass sound softer than 5ths and 8ves.

(7) Do not generally move further than a 3rd from the bass of a first inversion.

(8) Two positions of the same chord are good —∪.

(9) The bass of an inversion moving up a 2nd or 3rd to a root position, the melody moving in contrary motion and making the intervals 6 3 with the bass, is good. It is also good backwards.

(10) I*b* IV, and V*b* I are good when melody and bass move in consecutive 3rds. They are also good backwards.

(11) V*b* IV should be avoided.

(12) IV*b* V*b* is good. V*b* IV*b* is less common.

(13) An inverted cadence is good at the end of a subordinate phrase.

(14) I (or I*b*) IV is occasionally used at the end of a subordinate phrase.

(15) Inverted chords are often good at the beginning of a phrase.

## CHAPTER XI.

### Ib, IVb, Vb MINOR KEY

**1** AURAL AND VISUAL RECOGNITION. Fig. I shows I*b*, IV*b* and V*b* in C minor. Play them and listen to the effect. Maw is the bass note of I*b*, law of IV*b* and te of V*b*.

**Fig.1**

EAR TESTS. The teacher should play Ib, IV*b* and V*b* as isolated chords for recognition. Then he should add I, IV and V to the tests, so that the pupil learns to distinguish all the six chords from each other.

**Exercise I.** Play the following progressions, listening to the effect and naming the chords.

**Fig.2**

2 DOUBLING AND ARRANGEMENT. There is nothing new. Double the note that makes the smoothest and most correct part.

**Exercise II.** Harmonise the following melody and bass notes in the minor key. Make first inversions in every case.

Fig. 8

3 CHORD CHOICE. IV*b* and V*b* cannot be used together at present, as the bass notes make the interval of law–te. See Fig. 4.

Fig. 4

As the other first inversions are too far away from each other to sound well together, a 1st inversion in the minor key will always be preceded and followed by a root position, at present.

4 COMMON PROGRESSIONS TO BE PLAYED AND SUNG :—

Fig. 5

**Fig. 6**

EAR TESTS. A few specimen ear tests are given below. They may be played backwards also.

**Fig. 7**

**Exercise III.** Harmonise the following fragments, using one inversion and one root position in each case. Either root or inversion may come first.

**Fig. 8**

5 CADENCES. Fig. 9 shows some common cadences.

**Fig. 9**

EAR TESTS. The teacher should play cadences built from any chords known.

**Exercise 1V.** Write progressions of three chords, each progression ending with the following cadences, which may be inverted if you wish : (*a*) plagal in E minor ; (*b*) imperfect in C♯ minor ; (*c*) perfect in D minor ; (*d*) imperfect in B♭ minor ; (*e*) perfect in A minor.

6 HARMONISING MELODIES AND BASSES. Beware of augmented intervals, particularly when IV and V and their inversions occur next to each other. Look for opportunities of using common progressions.

**Exercise V.** Harmonise the following melodies :—

**Fig. 10**

**Exercise VI.** Harmonise the following basses :—

**Fig. 11**

7 FIGURED BASS. In the early seventeenth century a great change came over music. Instead of being thought of mainly in contrapuntal lines, it began to be thought of in block chords. The birth and rapid growth of opera hastened the process. Instead of many equally important voices singing a madrigal or motet, there was now a soloist in an opera, accompanied by subordinate orchestral instruments making a background of chords. The harpsichordist was the chief accompanist and he was given a bass part only, with figures underneath to show what chords he had to use. As long as he played the right chord, it did not matter how he arranged it.

This process was called " playing from figured bass " and musicians became very skilful at it.

Fig. 12 shows two short examples, one from Peri, one of the first opera composers, and one from Bach a hundred years later. Fig. 13 shows how the harpsichordist may perhaps have arranged them.

**Fig. 12**

**Fig. 13**

Later again, harmonies became more complex and composers began to be more particular about what was played, so they wrote what they wanted in full. Figured bass playing began to die out. But it persisted as a method of teaching harmony. A figured bass was given to a pupil and he had to fill in the parts. It was almost a kind of mathematics, and could be done equally well by the musical and unmusical, as no choice of chords, or hearing of the progressions was involved. Now this has almost died out. Nevertheless, figured bass is still useful as a kind of shorthand to indicate chords.

The intervals from the bass in a root position are $\frac{5}{3}$, and in a 1st inversion $\frac{6}{3}$. Root positions are so common that $\frac{5}{3}$ is generally implied, and so is the 3 in $\frac{6}{3}$. Fig. 14 (*a*) shows a figured bass using chords you know, and (*b*) shows a working of it.

**Fig. 14**

Figured bass is not, however, as good a shorthand as the Roman numerals, for a 6 underneath a bass note does not tell you the name of the chord, whereas V*b* does.

Accidentals required in harmonisation are also indicated in a figured bass. *E.g.*, ♯5 means sharpen the 5th from the bass note. ♯3 is generally written as ♯, and the 3 implied. An accidental is necessary under every V in a minor key because of te. One is also needed under I, if a Picardy 3rd is used.

**Exercise VII.** Harmonise the following figured basses. Write the Roman numerals under the bass according to the figuring used. Then continue as for an unfigured bass.

**Fig. 15**

SUMMARY OF RULES AND CHORD PROGRESSIONS.

(1) IV*b* and V*b* cannot be used next to each other in a minor key because the bass would be law te.

(2) Figured bass : Root position $=\binom{5}{3}$.

1st inversion $=\frac{6}{(3)}$.

Accidentals $= ♯6 ;  ♯(3)$.

# PART III

CHAPTER I.

SECONDARY TRIADS. VI AND II MAJOR KEY

(Paras. 1–7 are preliminaries. They state general principles which can then be applied to each new chord as it is learnt. They are intended to make a preliminary lesson in themselves. The teacher can, however, curtail them, or introduce them later, if he wishes.)

1 DEFINITION OF SECONDARY TRIADS. All diatonic triads which are not primary are called " secondary ". This means that II, III, VI and VII are secondary triads. You learnt in Part I, Chapter III that in a major key II, III and VI are minor triads and VII is a diminished triad. You also learnt to recognise them.

2 USES OF SECONDARY TRIADS. The main difference between primary and secondary triads is that the primary triads give a strong, clear impression of the tonality of the music, while the secondary triads are more vague and define the tonality less clearly. For this reason a judicious use of secondary among the more important primary triads gives the best effect.

Analyse and compare Fig. 1 (a), (b) and (c).

Fig. 1 a)

(*a*) rather lacks variety, though the tonality is clearly defined ; (*b*) sounds more like A minor than C major, the tonality is so vague ; (*c*) has plenty of variety, yet leaves us in no doubt of its key.

3 SECONDARY TRIADS AS AUXILIARIES TO PRIMARY TRIADS. Each primary triad can be thought of as having a kind of auxiliary triad a 3rd below it.

I = doh me soh ; VI = lah doh me. The melody notes doh and me, which the chords have in common, can sometimes be harmonised by VI, either instead of I, as at an interrupted cadence, or after I, to give variety. See Fig. 2 (*a*), (*b*) and (*c*).

Fig. 2   EWING

Similarly IV = fah lah doh ; II = ray fah lah. Fah and lah can be harmonised by II, either instead of IV, especially before V at a cadence, or after IV. See Fig. 3.

Similarly III is occasionally used in place of V.

This leaves VII unaccounted for. If V and VII are added together as at Fig. 4 (*a*) the dominant 7th, ⁷V, is produced.

In practice VII is so like V that it can be thought as an auxiliary to V, or even as an incomplete ⁷V. *e.g.*, VII*b* is often used instead of V at a cadence, as at Fig. 4 (*b*).

4 DOUBLING IN SECONDARY TRIADS. Doh, fah, and soh, the roots of the primary triads, are strong notes, and are generally doubled in these chords. But doh is the 3rd of VI, fah is the 3rd of II, and soh is the 3rd of III, so that doubling the 3rd of a secondary triad means doubling a strong note. Another reason for doing so is that II, III and VI are minor triads, and a minor 3rd can often be doubled more successfully than a major 3rd. Listen to the doublings in Fig. 5.

Fig. 5 a)    b)

This does not mean that the 3rd must always be doubled, but that it is done rather more frequently than in the primary triads, though it is still the exception to do so.

In VII te and fah (which make a diminished 5th) are such sensitive notes that they are better not doubled. So the 3rd, the strongest note, is nearly always doubled. See Fig. 4 (*b*).

5 MOVEMENT OF ROOTS. Some progressions of roots sound much better than others.

(*a*) Roots rising a 4th or falling a 5th (*i.e.*, reaching the same note at a different octave) make the strongest and most natural progression. You have already heard the effect in I IV and V I, and their inversions. It is very common with other chords also. Either chord may be inverted, but not both, as too great a leap would be made from the bass of a first inversion. Play and analyse Fig. 6. (*k*) and (*l*) show two discords ⁷V and ⁷II resolving in this way. It is the most normal method of resolving a discord.

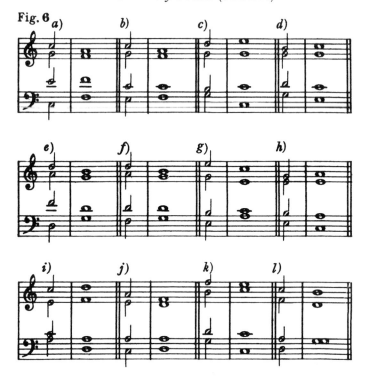

Fig. 6

(*b*) Roots rising a **5th** or falling a **4th** (*i.e.*, reaching the same note) are also very common. You already know I V, and IV I, and their inversions. Again, either chord can be inverted, but not both. Play and analyse Fig. 7.

Fig. 7

(c) Roots *falling* a 3rd, both chords being root positions, are good. If the roots *rise* a 3rd the progression is generally poor, as the second chord sounds strangely tame. See Fig. 8 (a) and (b). In both progressions the use of either or both chords inverted is awkward to manage, and sometimes ugly. So it is wise to avoid this at present. See (c) and (d). The best arrangements including inversions result when bass, tenor and alto are stationary and the melody moves 5 6 or 6 5. See (e), (f) and (g). In these cases the second note is rather like a passing note (your teacher can explain this term), and it is often as well to quit it by step. Whenever roots are a 3rd away from each other it is as well to move —∪, as the chords, having two notes in common, are so much alike.

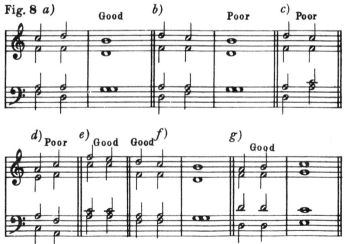

Fig. 8 a)

(*d*) Roots rising or falling a 2nd are sometimes very crude, and they are always difficult to manage, because of the risk of faulty consecutives.    IV V and V VI are the best root progressions of this kind, and II I is the worst.    Strangely enough, when both chords are inverted the result is always good.  The root is generally placed at the top and a different note is doubled in each chord, in order to avoid consecutives. Play and analyse Fig. 9.

(*e*) If roots move a 6th or 7th the chords reached are the same as if they had moved a 3rd or 2nd.  But basses do not generally move so far.

6 EXPOSED 5THS AND 8VES.  You have learnt that exposed 5ths and 8ves do not sound wrong if the top part moves by step.  Be careful, however, when dealing with secondary triads, as exposed 5ths and 8ves are apt, even under these conditions, to stand out.  It may be wiser not to write them at all, if either or both chords concerned are secondary triads.  See Fig. 10.

**Fig. 10**

**Exercise I.** Play and then analyse Figs. 11 (*a*) and (*b*). State the following facts about each chord : (1) its name ; (2) which note is doubled ; (3) the interval the root makes with the root of the next chord and whether either or both chords are inverted. See how these facts bear out paras. 2–5.

**Fig. 11** *a)*

*b)*

**Exercise II.** Name the chords implied in the following figured basses and analyse the movement of the roots. Then fill in alto and tenor, doubling the note which makes the smoothest and most correct movement.

**Fig. 12**

7 PARTICULAR USES OF SECONDARY TRIADS. III is an awkward chord, and is so rarely used that you might look through pages of music without finding an instance of it. Its treatment is deferred until Part V.

VII is a discord, and is therefore left over for the present. II and VI will now be considered.

8 II V (root rising a 4th). II, and its inversion II*b*, are more used than any other chords before V at a cadence. Aurally, the main difficulty is to distinguish II from IV, whose auxiliary it is. (See para. 3.) Listen for ray and a leap to soh in the bass. Fig. 13 shows some common uses of each progression for comparison.

Notice that melody and bass have moved in contrary motion to each other in every example. This is not imperative, but it generally sounds best.

9 II V*b*. II often moves to V*b*. The bass is smoother than it is in moving to V, but the result is not so strong. Listen for te in the bass. See Fig. 14. (*a*) is the most common arrangement, with the melody moving in contrary motion to the bass, and making the intervals 3 6 (Cf. with other progressions such as I IV*b*, and V I*b*, which have been treated similarly).

10 II—OTHER KNOWN CHORDS. II *can* move to other chords already known, but rarely does so, and it is more difficult to make the progression sound natural. II I is ugly (roots a 2nd apart), II IV sounds tame (root rising a 3rd). See Fig. 15 (*a*) and (*b*). It sometimes moves to VI, however, (root rising a 5th) and as you will shortly be learning **VI**, this progression is illustrated in Fig. 15 (*c*) and (*d*).

**Fig. 15**

11 APPROACHES TO II.  IV, V, and VI all lead well to II (roots falling a 3rd, 4th, and 5th respectively). Their inversions do not move as naturally to II, on the whole. I II is ugly. Play and analyse Fig. 16. Notice that in V II te rises, though not to doh.

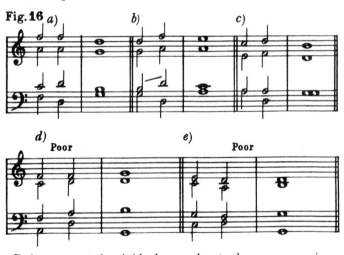

**Fig. 16**

Rules cannot be laid down about these progressions, however. A good bass line and good movement between melody and bass are the best tests of chord choice, and your developing aural sense should guide you as much as possible.

EQUAL VOICES.  Fig. 17 shows some of the more common progressions including II, arranged for equal voices.

**Fig. 17**

EAR TESTS. The teacher should first give ear tests contrasting IV with II, as in Fig. 12. Then II should be contained in progressions of three chords, common arrangements of known chords being used in every case.

**Exercise III.** Write (*a*) II V I ; (*b*) II V*b* I ; (*c*) IV II V in the keys of F, A♭ and B major.

**Exercise IV.** Harmonise the following fragments, using II once in each case.

**Fig. 18**

12 V VI (root rising a 2nd). The most frequent use of V VI is at an interrupted cadence. Like the inverted cadence it is a useful means of avoiding too final an effect at the end of a subordinate phrase, or before a slight break. Play Fig. 19 (*a*)–(*c*). (*a*) is by far the most common arrangement.

**Fig. 19**

There is once more a danger of faulty consecutives caused by parallel motion (see Fig. 19 (*d*)), and as in the case of IV V, and IV*b* V*b*, the remedy is again contrary movement. This time the solution is to double the 3rd in VI. Cf. Fig. 19 (*a*) with (*d*). It is, as previously mentioned, a strong primary note. (The 3rd must also be doubled in VI if the progression is used backwards, VI V.)

13 I VI (root falling a 3rd). Look again at Fig. 2 (*c*) for common instances of this progression. Fig. 20 gives further examples. There is no special need to double the 3rd in VI.

**Fig. 20** *a)*     *b)*     *c)*     *d)*     *e)*

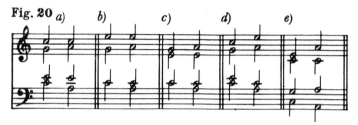

14 II VI (root rising a 5th). This progression has already been mentioned in para. 10 and illustrated in Fig. 15 (*c*) and (*d*).

15 VI FROM OTHER KNOWN CHORDS. Although other arrangements are possible, you are advised to keep to the above progressions most of the time. IV VI is root rising a 3rd, I*b* VI is a big leap from the bass of a 1st inversion, and so on. IV*b* VI is occasionally used as at Fig. 8 (*e*), the melody making the intervals 6 5 with the bass.

16 QUITTING OF VI. Notice that in dealing with II we first discussed the movements from it, while with VI we have first discussed the approaches to it. This aptly illustrates the difference between the two chords. II is generally leading somewhere. VI often occurs at the end of a phrase, or there is a slight break after it. If it comes at a break the next chord will probably be V or IV. If it comes in the middle of a phrase the next chord is frequently V, IV, or II, but it may be any known chord except I and I*b* (roots rising a 3rd). Play and analyse Fig. 21. All the examples are satisfactory.

**Fig. 21**

Equal voice arrangements introducing VI :—

**Fig. 22**

EAR TESTS. The teacher should compare the interrupted with the other cadences, and also give progressions of three chords, including VI in its most common contexts and arrangements.

**Exercise V.** Write progressions of three chords ending with an interrupted cadence in the keys of A, B♭ and E major. Do not anticipate the cadence by using VI on the previous strong accent.

**Exercise VI.** Harmonise the following fragments, using VI once in each example :—

**Fig. 23**

17 BEGINNINGS AND ENDINGS OF PHRASES. The first two and last two chords of a phrase should generally be primary triads or their inversions, so as to keep the tonality clear. There are three exceptions :—

(*a*) I VI is a common beginning.

(*b*) V VI is a common ending.

(*c*) A secondary triad, *e.g.*, II may be the penultimate chord if followed by V in an imperfect cadence.

V should generally be introduced not later than the fourth chord of phrase, if the tonality is to be clear. Cf. Fig 1 (*a*) and (*c*) with (*b*).)

18 HARMONISING MELODIES AND BASSES. Use only 1, 1*b*, IV, IV*b*, V, V*b*, II and VI. Think in progressions. When in doubt about a chord analyse the movement of the roots.

**Exercise VII.** Harmonise the following melodies :—

Fig. 24

**Exercise VIII.** Harmonise the following basses. The first two are figured, the rest unfigured.

SUMMARY OF RULES AND CHORD PROGRESSIONS.

(1) The 3rd of a secondary triad can be doubled more freely than the 3rd of a primary triad.

(2) Roots moving a 4th and 5th are good when both chords are in root position or when one chord is inverted.

(3) Roots moving a 3rd, both chords being root positions, are good when falling, and poor when rising. If either or both chords are inverted, both progressions are awkward to manage and are rather rare. Chords having two notes in common are better —◡.

(4) Roots moving a 2nd are always awkward to manage and are rarely good. IV V and V VI are the best of these progressions. If both chords are inverted the

effect is always good, provided that a different note is doubled in each chord. The root is generally in the melody.

(5) Avoid exposed 5ths and 8ves when either or both chords concerned are secondary triads.

(6) II moves frequently to V, sometimes to V*b* or VI, rarely to other chords.

(7) IV, V and VI can all lead to II.

(8) VI is generally preceded by V or I or II.

(9) VI is frequently followed by V, IV or II, but other chords are possible.

(10) In using V VI or VI V double the 3rd in VI.

(11) Establish the key clearly at the beginnings and ends of phrases.

## CHAPTER II

## VI, MINOR KEY

1 SECONDARY TRIADS OF THE MINOR KEY. Refer to Part I, Chapter V. You will see that in a minor key II and VII are diminished triads, III is augmented, and VI is major. As the treatment of diminished and augmented triads is deferred until Part V, the only addition to the vocabulary at the moment is VI.

2 V VI. The 3rd is doubled in VI, as in the major key, and for the same reason. Notice that this means doubling the 3rd of a major chord. In the major key VI is minor, in the minor key it is major. See Fig. 1.

**Fig. 1**

3 I VI. I is the only other known chord which is frequently used before VI in a minor key, as II cannot be used at all. See Fig. 2.

**Fig. 2**

4 QUITTING OF VI. As in the major key, V and IV are the most usual chords after a cadence ending with VI. IV,

IV*b* and V are the only chords which can follow VI in a minor key. Decide for yourself why I, I*b* and V*b* cannot do so.

**Fig. 8**

Equal voice arrangements introducing VI :—

**Fig. 4**

EAR TESTS. As in the major key.

**Exercise I.** Write progressions of three chords ending with an interrupted cadence, in the keys of C, F, and E minor.

**Exercise II.** Harmonise the following fragments, in the minor key, using VI once in each example :—

**Fig. 5**

5 PHRASING. In future, the phrasing of exercises will not be given. Sing the exercise through and add the phrasing for yourself. You will have learnt about phrasing in aural

lessons and in connection with melody writing. A few points are mentioned here :

(*a*) A melody in 2 or 3 time frequently has four bar phrases, while one in 4 time or slow $\frac{6}{8}$ time frequently has two bar phrases.

(*b*) If one phrase begins (*e.g.*) on the 3rd beat of the bar the other phrases are very likely to begin on the 3rd beat also.

(*c*) A phrase is frequently broken up into smaller sections, particularly when sequences are being used.

If you phrase wrongly your harmonies will be wrong.

6 HARMONISING MELODIES AND BASSES. The chords at your disposal in the minor key are I, I*b*, IV, IV*b*, V, V*b* and VI.

**Exercise III.** Harmonise the following melodies :—

**Fig. 6**

**Exercise IV.** Harmonise the following figured and un-figured basses :—

SUMMARY OF CHORD PROGRESSIONS.

(1)  II cannot be used in the minor key (at present).

(2)  VI is used as in the major key.

### IIb, VIIb, and VIb MAJOR KEY

1 1ST INVERSIONS OF SECONDARY TRIADS, MAJOR KEY. You have learnt a little about these chords in Part I, Chapter III, paras. 5–10, and you can recognise them in isolation.

We shall defer consideration of IIIb, as like III, it is rare.

2 IIb V (root rising a 4th). As mentioned in Part III, Chapter I, II and IIb are very common before V, at a cadence. IIb is perhaps less strong than II, but the movement of the bass is smoother. It is more frequently used than II. Play and analyse Fig. 1. (a) is very common. Notice the familiar contrary motion between the outside parts, making the intervals 6 3. (b) is rather rare, and (c) is hardly ever used. IIb nearly always has the root at the top.

**Fig. 1** *a)*     *b)*     *c)*

3 IIb TO OTHER CHORDS. Make a list of all the chords you know, and decide which will follow IIb well, applying what you already know about chord choice. Then compare your list with that given below, and play the examples in Fig. 2. Do not attempt to memorise the list, but follow the reasoning.

IIb I   Root falling a 2nd ; leap of 4th from bass of 1st inversion ; rare.

IIb Ib   Root falling a 2nd ; consecutive 1st inversions ; good with the roots at the top.

IIb II   Two positions of the same chord ; good —∪.

IIb IV   Root rising a 3rd, bass note the same ; good if melody 6 5, and chords —∪.

II*b* IV*b*   Root rising a 3rd ; poor.
II*b* V*b*    Root rising a 4th, both chords inverted ; poor.
II*b* VI     Root rising a 5th, one chord inverted ; good.
II*b* VI*b*   Root rising a 5th, both chords inverted ; poor.

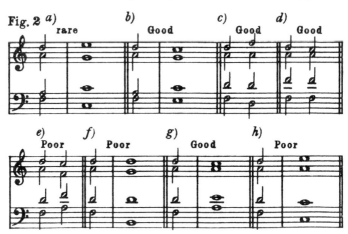

4 II*b* FROM OTHER CHORDS. Make a similar list of chords which lead well to II*b*. Then write examples from the list. As there are many good chords, there is no need to remember particular progressions. I II*b* is fairly common, in spite of the roots being a 2nd apart.

As mentioned in para. 2, II*b* is rarely used with the 5th at the top. If it is used thus after I*b*, it sounds as if it contains a wrong note. IV is the natural chord in such a place. Cf. Fig. 3 (*a*) and (*c*) with (*b*) and (*d*).

CHORD SINGING. (a)–(d) can also be sung backwards :—

Fig. 4 a) b) c) d)

e) f)

EAR TESTS. The teacher should contrast II, IIb and IV before V at a cadence. IIb and IV are very much alike. The pupil should listen for ray. Then progressions of three or four chords, including IIb, should be played.

**Exercise I.** Write IIb V I in keys F, A, and B♭ major.

**Exercise II.** Harmonise the following fragments, using IIb once in each case :—

Fig. 5 a) b) c)

d) e) f) g)

h) i) j)

5 VIb. This chord has a vagueness which makes it most useful for modulating purposes (see Fig. 6 (a)), but dangerous otherwise. Unless using it next to its own root position, it is wiser not to leap to or from it at present. Place the root at the top.

It can move to or from : (*a*) II, root moving a 4th, outside parts moving in contrary motion and making the intervals 6 3, Fig. 6 (*b*) ; V*b* or VII*b*, consecutive 1st inversions, with the root at the top, Fig. 6 (*c*) and (*d*) ; (*c*) its own root position VI, Fig. 6 (*e*). Do not use it elsewhere, and, in any case, use it sparingly.

**Fig. 6** *a)*          *b)*

*c)*        *d)*                    *e)*

CHORD SINGING.

**Fig. 7** *a)*          *b)*          *c)*

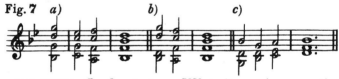

EAR TESTS. Confine tests on VI*b* to its use in connection with II, V*b*, VII*b* and VI.

**Exercise III.** Harmonise the following fragments, using VI*b* once in each case.

**Fig. 8** *a)*                    *b)*

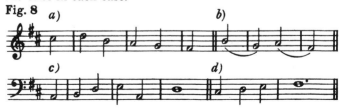

*c)*                    *d)*

6 VII*b*. Although VII*b* is a concord and is frequently used, there are only three progressions in which it normally occurs. See paras. 7, 8 and 9. Remember that the 3rd is generally doubled.

7 I VII*b* I*b* AND BACKWARDS. This is a very common progression. Melody and bass frequently move in contrary motion,

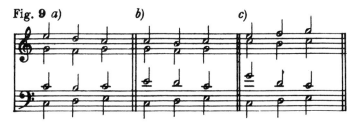

are sometimes found in the melody. Play all the progressions in Fig. 9 backwards also. VII*b* has the effect of being a passing or link chord between two positions of I, so it should occur on a weak beat.

**Fig. 9** *a)*            *b)*            *c)*

In this progression we meet a perfect followed by a diminished 5th for the first time. Can you hear anything ugly in Fig. 9 (*a*) ? The 5ths are quite satisfactory, provided that they are not with the bass (which they cannot be, at present).

8 VII*b* I OR VI AT A CADENCE. Think of the VII*b* as replacing V. The root is generally at the top. Make the progression move as smoothly as possible.

**Fig. 10** *a)*            *b)*

9 VII*b* VI*b* OR I*b* (consecutive 1st inversions). Notice the doubling and the fact that the roots are at the top.

Fig. 11

CHORD SINGING.

Fig. 12

EAR TESTS. Confine ear tests on VII*b* to the uses given above.

**Exercise IV.** Harmonise the following fragments, using VII*b* once in each case :—

Fig. 13

10 HARMONISING MELODIES AND BASSES. Every diatonic triad in its root position and 1st inversion, except III, III*b*, and VII, can now be used.

Adding alto and tenor should by now have become an easy process. So it should not be necessary to fill in the inner parts in every exercise in future. But always indicate the chords by Roman numerals.

**Exercise V.** Harmonise the following melodies :—

**Exercise VI.** Harmonise the following figured and un-figured basses :—

SUMMARY OF RULES AND CHORD PROGRESSIONS.

(1) II*b* V is very common at a cadence.

(2) II*b* may move to or from a number of chords.

(3) II*b* and VI*b* generally have the root at the top.

(4) The bass of VI*b* generally moves by step, except when moving to its own root position. It can move to II, V*b*, VII*b* or VI. Use it sparingly.

(5) The 3rd is generally doubled in VII*b*.

(6) VII*b* is frequently used in the following progressions :—

    (*a*) I VII*b* I*b* and backwards ; (*b*) VII*b* I or VI at a cadence ; (*c*) VII*b* VI*b* or I*b* (consecutive 1st inversions).

(7) A perfect and diminished 5th may follow each other, provided that they are not with the bass.

1 1ST INVERSION OF SECONDARY TRIADS IN THE MINOR KEY. In the last chapter it was explained that VIIb in the major key can be used, because the first inversion of a diminished triad is a concord. This also applies to IIb and VIIb in a minor key.

The use of IIb, VIb and VIIb in the minor key corresponds so closely to their use in the major, that the best method of studying them is to compare the two chapters. The paragraph and figure numbers have purposely been kept the same, and all major key examples and exercises which sound well in the minor are here reproduced in the tonic minor. Progressions which include II or produce augmented intervals cannot be used. Work as follows :—

(a) Read a paragraph of the major chapter and play the examples.

(b) Turn the examples into the tonic minor and decide which can be used.

(c) Test your conclusions by referring to the corresponding paragraph and examples in this chapter.

2 IIb V. See Fig. 1.

3 IIb TO OTHER CHORDS. Fig. 2 of the previous chapter gave good and bad progressions. The best in the minor key are given here. IIb rarely moves to VI in the minor key.

Fig. 2

4 IIb FROM OTHER CHORDS. As in the major key, Ib IV
sounds better than Ib IIb in Fig. 3.

Fig. 8   *a)* Good   *b)* Bad   *c)* Good   *d)* Bad

CHORD SINGING.

Fig.4

EAR TESTS. As in the major key.
**Exercise I.** Write IIb V I in keys F, A, and B♮ minor.
**Exercise II.** Harmonise the following, fragments using
IIb once in each case.

Fig.5

**5 VI***b***.** In the minor key VI*b* is exceedingly rare. It sounds very remote from the key, and is difficult to precede and follow. V*b* and VI are the best chords to use next to it. It may be advisable for you to avoid its use in a minor key altogether.

Fig. 6

CHORD SINGING. See Fig. 7.

Fig. 7

EAR TESTS. As in the major key.

**Exercise III.** None of the exercises given in the major key chapter will work in the minor. Harmonise the following fragments, using VI*b* once in each case :—

Fig. 8

**6 VII***b***.** This chord is identical in the major and minor key.

**7 I VII***b* I***b***. See Fig. 9.

Fig. 9    a)        b)        c)

8 VII*b* I AT A CADENCE.    (VII*b* cannot move to VI in a minor key.)    See Fig. 10.

Fig. 10    a)

9 VII*b* I*b* (consecutive 1st inversions). (VII*b* rarely moves to VI*b*, as augmented intervals almost inevitably ensue.)

Fig. 11    a)        b)

CHORD SINGING.

Fig 12    a)        b)        c)        e)

EAR TESTS. As in the major key.

**Exercise IV.** Harmonise the following fragments, using VII*b* once in each case :—

Fig. **13**

10 HARMONISING MELODIES AND BASSES. In the minor key every diatonic triad in its root position and first inversion, with the exceptions of II, III, III*b*, and VII, can be used.

**Exercise V.** Harmonise the following melodies :—

Fig. **14**

**Exercise VI.** Harmonise the following figured and unfigured basses :—

Fig. **15**

SUMMARY OF RULES AND CHORD PROGRESSIONS.

(1) II*b* cannot move to II (at present) and rarely moves to VI in a minor key.

(2) VI*b* is rare in the minor key. V*b* and VI are the best chords to use next to it.

(3) VII*b* cannot move to VI or VI*b* in a minor key.

## CHAPTER V.

### TWO PART WRITING. NOTE AGAINST NOTE

1 TWO PART WRITING. There are four essentials in good two part writing, viz. :—

(*a*) Each part must be melodically interesting.

(*b*) The two parts must be sufficiently contrasted for them to be clearly heard as individual parts.

(*c*) The two parts must make satisfactory intervals with each other.

(*d*) The two parts must imply good harmony.

Each point will now be considered separately.

2 MELODIC MOVEMENT. In the four part harmony you have been writing, it has been a virtue to repeat a note in a melodic part, and even to move round the same notes, except perhaps in the soprano. But when there are only two parts they must be as melodically interesting as possible. Repeated notes should be sparingly used, and each part should have a good curve and lead to a climax if possible. There should also be some rhythmic variety, though you are limited in this respect at present. Augmented intervals and awkward leaps should still be avoided, and stepwise movement should predominate.

3 CONTRAST BETWEEN THE PARTS. Parts which are in contrast to each other are much easier to hear as separate parts, and provide more interest to the listener. Contrasted rhythm and contrary motion help considerably. Unfortunately you cannot use contrasted rhythm yet, as you will first learn to write the same note lengths in both parts, *i.e.*, "note against note". But use as much contrary motion as possible. Fig. 1 (*a*) is better than (*b*).

**Fig. 1** *a)*      *b)*

4 INTERVALS BETWEEN THE PARTS. At present the two parts must be concordant with each other. This means that only perfect unisons, 5ths and 8ves, and major and minor 3rds and 6ths can be used. Remember that the 4th is discordant if sounded with the bass, and that the lowest part heard, even if it is the alto, is considered to be the bass.

5 PERFECT CONCORDS (1sts, 5ths and 8ves). Use these sparingly, as they are bare, and there are no inner parts to soften them. They are always good (*a*) at the beginning or end of an exercise. See Fig. 2 (*a*) ; (*b*) if other notes of the same implied chord are used before or after, so that a broken chord effect is suggested. See Fig. 2 (*b*). At other times use them as smoothly as possible and generally by contrary motion, so that they do not stand out. Use them on a weak beat in preference to a strong one. See Fig. 2 (*c*). The rule about exposed 5ths and 8ves of course applies, also the rule about consecutive 5ths and 8ves. Fig. 2 (*d*) shows a 5th approached by similar motion, but between primary triads with the top part moving by step.

**Fig. 2**

6 IMPERFECT CONCORDS (3rds and 6ths). Use these as much as possible, but do not write a succession of consecutive 3rds or 6ths, as the parts are not then independent. Play Fig. 2 again, noticing the use of the imperfect concords.

7 IMPLIED HARMONY. The two parts are meant to sound complete in themselves, but nevertheless complete chords are implied, and if this implied chord succession is not good, then the effect of the two parts is not good. You must only imply chords you have learnt, hence the restriction to concords. A 5th from the bass implies a root position, a 6th implies a first inversion. A 3rd and an 8ve may imply either.

Fig. 3 shows two workings of the same bass. Both use allowable intervals, and have no grammatical errors. Play them without looking at the names of the implied chords. Then analyse the harmony, and you will realise why (*a*) sounds so much better than (*b*).

**Fig. 3**

A 6th followed by a 3rd in contrary motion and *vice versa* is very common, and implies harmonic progressions you have frequently used. Play Fig. 4 naming all the implied chords. In every case the second chord implied is a root position, as you will realise if you fill in the alternative harmonies as in Fig. 5. All the examples in Fig. 4 are good backwards.

Fig. 4

a)    b)    c)    d)

e)    f)    g)

Fig. 5

a) 1. Good    a) 2. Bad    b) 1. Good

I    VIb    II

b) 2. Bad    c) 1. Good    c) 2. Bad

VIIb    IV    IIb

8 SPACING. The parts may be close together, or as much as two or three octaves apart, according to the voices for which they are written. When writing for soprano and bass do not try to leave room for an imaginary alto and tenor, as the two parts are complete in themselves.

9 IMITATION AND SEQUENCE. These devices are useful for creating interest. The added part may enter after the given part and imitate it, as in Fig. 6 (*a*) and (*b*). But do not let a part entering on a weak beat be imitated on a strong beat, or *vice versa*. See Fig. 6 (*c*). Such an entry is poor rhythmically, even if imitation is not being used.

**Fig. 6**

A sequence is good, providing that it is not repeated too often. One repetition is generally sufficient, and even this need not be identical. See the melody of Fig. 7 (*a*) and (*b*). The added part generally has a sequence also, but is not bound to do so. See the bass parts in Fig. 7.

**Fig. 7**

10 METHOD OF HARMONISING A MELODY IN TWO PARTS.

(1) Sing the melody to sol-fa.
(2) Add the phrase marks.
(3) Add Roman numerals and a bass. Follow the rules of good chord progression. Use concords only, and imperfect in preference to perfect ones, particularly on the accent. Use contrary motion as much as possible, and get a good melodic line. If in doubt about a note or two, leave a gap and go on to a part which suggests something definite, filling in the gap afterwards.
(4) Sing the bass to sol-fa and check it.
(5) Try to hear the two parts together, and check them.
(6) Play or sing the final result.

**Exercise I.** Add interesting basses to the following melodies, writing note against note :—

Fig. 8

*Let the bass enter here.

11 METHOD OF HARMONISING A BASS IN TWO PARTS.

(1) Sing the bass to sol-fa.

(2) Add the phrase marks.

(3) Write Roman numerals under the bass. If you are not sure about a note, or you think two chords are equally good, write both names down. At present the bass note can only be the root or 3rd of a chord. See Fig. 9.

**Fig. 9**

(4) From this harmonic scheme write a melody. Use imperfect concords (particularly on the accent) and contrary motion as much as possible. Get a good melodic line. If in doubt about a note or two, leave a gap and go on to a part which suggests something definite, filling in the gap afterwards. See Fig. 10.

**Fig. 10**

(5) Sing the melody to sol-fa and check it.
(6) Try to hear the two parts together and check them.
(7) Play or sing the final result.

**Exercise II**. Add interesting melodies to the following basses :—

**Fig. 11**

*Let the soprano enter here. Notice that the top part generally dictates the length of the phrase.

12 MINOR KEY. Two part writing in the minor key follows the same principles as that in the major. But remember that augmented intervals cannot be used melodically, and that neither diminished nor augmented intervals can be used harmonically (in two part writing) at present, as they are discords and imply chords not yet learnt.

**Exercise III.** Add interesting basses to the following melodies :—

**Fig. 12**

**Exercise IV.** Add interesting melodies to the following basses :—

**Fig.13**

EAR TESTS. Short two part exercises, using the resources of this chapter, should be dictated.

SUMMARY OF RULES.

(1) Each part must be interesting, have a good curve and, if possible, a climax.

(2) The parts must be as contrasted as possible. Use plenty of contrary motion.

(3) Perfect concords should be used sparingly.
  They are good :—
   (a) at the beginning and end ;
   (b) before or after another position of the same chord ;
   (c) used smoothly and approached by contrary motion ;
   (d) approached by similar motion between primary triads, if the top part moves by step.
  Use them on a weak beat in preference to a strong one.

(4) Use plenty of imperfect concords, but do not write a succession of consecutive 3rds and 6ths.

(5) The two parts must imply good harmony.

(6) Imitation and sequence are useful devices for creating interest.

14

# PART IV

# UNESSENTIAL NOTES AND DISCORDS

## CHAPTER I.

### MELODIC DECORATION

1 THE DIFFERENCE BETWEEN ELEMENTARY HARMONY AND COMPOSITION. If you examine a work by, *e.g.*, Mozart or Beethoven you will find—perhaps to your surprise—that these composers do not use a great many chords which you have not learnt, but that they use simple harmonies with a great deal of decoration. Look at Fig. 1:—

**Fig. 1**

SONATA IN G                                                    *Mozart*

The chord scheme of the above passage is simple, but delightfully varied decoration is used, and the result is artistically satisfying. It is the use of decoration rather than a wider harmonic vocabulary, that accounts for the main technical difference between elementary harmony, and composition.

This chapter explains various kinds of decoration. It is not intended that they should all be made use of in harmony exercises at this stage, but, they should be understood, so that they can be recognised. The harmonic basis of a composition can then be grasped, sight reading becomes much easier, and the understanding of composers' ideas steadily grows.

2 CHORD RHYTHM. Without decoration, it is very dull for one chord to last any length of time, and so the chords are changed nearly every beat as, *e.g.*, in hymn tunes and the exercises which you have been writing. But when decorations are added, the chords do not need to move so frequently. A chord rhythm of one chord a bar is of very common occurrence. See Fig. 1 above.

3 DECORATION. Two main kinds of decoration are possible, viz. :—

(1) Decoration with " essential " notes, *i.e.*, notes of the chord, whether concords or discords.

(2) Decoration with " unessential " notes, *i.e.*, notes which do not belong to the chord.

In the following paragraphs examples of each type are shown, decorating the chord scheme I, IV, V, I.

4 ESSENTIAL NOTES. Chord notes are useful for decoration, provided that they do not move too quickly to be singable.

**Fig. 2**

I        IV        V        I

At a quicker rate they are apt to sound fussy unless interspersed with unessential notes, owing to the disjunct movement. It is a general principle that the quicker a part moves the smoother it should run. Otherwise it becomes unsingable. See Fig. 3 :—

**Fig. 3**

If a part is not meant to be melodic, but consists of, *e.g.*, brilliant arpeggios written for the piano, then the principle does not apply.

**Fig. 4**

PIANO CONCERTO IN C MINOR                                    *Beethoven*

**Exercise I.** Write melodies over the following chord schemes, using essential notes throughout. Aim at a varied rhythm. (The chord schemes in *Exercises I* to *VI* are meant to employ one chord a bar.)

(1) *Minuet.* $\frac{3}{4}$ I, IV, I, V ; I, IV, V, I.

(2) *March.* $\frac{4}{4}$ I, IV, II, V ; VI, IV, V, I.

5 UNESSENTIAL NOTES. There are several types of unessential notes. They are summarised in paras. 6 to 9.

6 PASSING NOTES. Unessential notes which are used scale-wise (*i.e.*, by step upwards or downwards) and which join two chord notes, are called passing notes. There are two kinds, unaccented and accented. See Fig. 5 (*a*) and (*b*) :—

**Fig. 5**

They cannot leap to or from a note (Fig. 6 (*a*) and (*d*)) nor can they remain where they are (Fig. 6 (*c*)). They must " pass ". If they start upwards they must continue upwards by step until they reach another harmony note, and *vice versa*. They cannot change their direction, as at Fig. 6 (*b*).

**Fig. 6**

Fig. 6 is quite satisfactory, but the notes marked are not passing notes.

Passing notes occasionally move in semitones, *e.g.*, C, C♯ D, D♯, E, thus using chromatic notes, but this kind can be ignored for the present.

**Exercise II.** Write melodies over the following chord schemes, using essential and passing notes only :—

(1) *March.* $\frac{2}{4}$ I, VI, IV, V ; I, IV, V, I.
(2) *Cradle Song.* $\frac{6}{8}$ I, IV, V, I.

7 AUXILIARY NOTES. Every chord note has, as its auxiliaries, the scale note above and the tone and semitone below. Like passing notes, they can be unaccented, or accented. Several decorative figures can be built with them, and as ornaments are largely built up of auxiliary notes, some of these figures can borrow their names. Ornaments are often played more quickly than the decorations quoted here, but this does not affect the nomenclature.

(*a*) *Mordent* (◡). This consists of a chord note, the scale note above and the same chord note again. (A *trill* (tr) uses the same notes, but repeats the figure as many times as possible.)

**Fig. 7**

(b) *Lower mordent* (𝄍). This consists of a chord note, the tone or semitone below, and the same chord note again. The semitone is rather more common in modern music. Use whichever you prefer in the context.

**Fig. 8**

(c) *Turn* (∞). This consists of a chord note, the scale note above, the same chord note, the tone or semitone below, and the same chord note again. Sometimes the first chord note is left out. In the inverted turn ∞ or ? the lower auxiliary note comes first.

**Fig. 9**

(d) *Changing note figure*. This is like the turn, with the chord note in the middle left out. It can also occur when the chord notes are a 3rd apart. Its essential feature is the leap of a 3rd in the middle, between two auxiliary notes.

**Fig. 10**

(e) *An auxiliary note between two chord notes a step apart.* This also has a leap of a 3rd in the middle.

**Fig. 11**

(*f*) *An auxiliary note approached by leap, unaccented.* This is rather rare. It is quitted by step on to the chord note ot which it is an auxiliary.

**Fig. 12**

   I                IV         V                I

(*g*) *Appoggiatura.* This is the accented form of (*f*) above. It is of frequent occurrence.

**Fig. 13**

   I                IV         V                I

At one time appoggiaturas were written thus : ♪♩ , so that the chord note should easily be recognised. Fig. 14 shows how Fig. 13 would look if written in this way.

**Fig. 14**

   I                IV         V                I

(*h*) *Acciaccatura.* This is similar to an appoggiatura, but it is played as quickly as possible. It is written thus : ♪♩

**Exercise III.** Write melodies over the following chord schemes, making use of any auxiliary note figures, except appoggiaturas and acciaccaturas :—

(1) *Waltz.* $\frac{3}{4}$ I, IV, I, V ; VI, II, V, I.

(2) *Galop.* $\frac{2}{4}$ I, V, I, IV ; I, VI, V, I.

**Exercise IV.** Write melodies over the following chord schemes, making use of appoggiaturas and acciaccaturas :—

(1) *Funeral March.* $\frac{4}{4}$ I, VI, II, V ; V, VI, IV, I.

(2) *Waltz.* $\frac{3}{4}$ I, IV, II, V ; V, VI, V, I.

8 SUSPENSIONS. Imagine a melodic part which falls by step from an essential note of one chord to an essential note of the next (different) chord. See the Soprano part of **Fig. 15 (*a*).**

**Fig. 15**

If the first note is held on while the rest of the chord moves, as at Fig. 15 (*b*), a " suspension " is heard as an unessential note against the second chord. It afterwards falls by step to the second chord note. Occasionally the movement is by step upwards instead of downwards. See Fig. 15 (*c*). The suspension is then sometimes called a " retardation ".

**Fig. 16**

Notice that :—

    (*a*) An accented passing note is *approached by step* and quitted by step.

    (*b*) An appoggiatura is *approached by leap* and quitted by step.

    (*c*) A suspension is *approached from the same note* and quitted by step.

           They all occur on an accent.

As there is a danger of confusing these three, look again at Figs 5 (*b*), 13 and 16.

Notice also that a repeated or tied note is not necessarily a suspension. It may be a syncopated chord note. See Fig. 17. A suspension must be unessential when heard against the second chord.

**Fig. 17**

**Exercise V.** Write melodies over the following chord schemes, making use of suspensions :—

(1) *Sarabande.* $\frac{3}{4}$ I, IV, II, VI ; V, I*b*, V, I.

(2) *Cradle Song.* $\frac{3}{8}$ I, IV, V, VI ; V, I*b*, VII*b*, I.

9 ANTICIPATIONS. When two chord notes move by step the second may be anticipated over the harmony of the first. This device of anticipation is primarily a vocal one, being sometimes used when a word begins with a weak syllable.

**Fig. 18**

Spring comes a - gain, Oh let us a - way
I        IV      V      I

**Exercise VI.** Write melodies over the following chord schemes, making use of anticipations :—

(1) *Gigue.* $\frac{9}{8}$ I, IV, II, V ; I, IV, V, I.

(2) *Folk Song.* $\frac{4}{4}$ I, V, I, IV ; I, VI, V, I.

10 DECORATION IN COMPOSITION. In actual composition all these decorations are freely intermingled. Fig. 19 shows an example from Beethoven's piano concerto in C minor. The whole of this work might well be analysed from a decorative point of view, as the harmonic scheme is generally seen clearly in the orchestral part (piano arrangement).

**Fig. 19**

Key to the above : (*a*) Chord note ; (*b*) unaccented passing note ; (*c*) accented passing note ; (*d*) auxiliary note ; (*e*) appoggiatura ; (*f*) suspension.

**Exercise VII.** What kind of decoration is illustrated in each of the following passages ?

**Fig. 20**

PIANO CONCERTO IN C MINOR *Beethoven*

**Exercise VIII.** Name the kind of note which occurs at the beginning of every beat in the melody in Fig. 21.

**Fig. 21**

PIANO CONCERTO IN C MINOR *Beethoven*

SUMMARY OF RULES.

1 Decoration can consist of essential and unessential notes.

2 Essential notes are chord notes (whether concords or discords).

3 Unessential notes do not belong to the chord. There are four main types :—

(*a*) *Passing notes* (accented and unaccented) which must move by step in the same direction, from chord note to chord note.

(*b*) *Auxiliary notes* (accented and unaccented) which are the notes above and below the chord note. They are used in the following figures :—

(1) Mordent ; (2) lower mordent ; (3) turn ; (4) changing note ; (5) an auxiliary note between two chord notes a step apart ; (6) an auxiliary note approached by leap ; (7) appoggiatura ; (8) acciaccatura.

(*c*) *Suspensions*, which occur on the accent and are approached from the same note in the previous chord, afterwards falling (occasionally rising) by step to the next chord note.

(*d*) *Anticipations*, which occur off the accent, and anticipate a chord note over the previous chord, being then repeated as their chord is sounded.

## CHAPTER II.

### DECORATED TWO PART WRITING.  MAJOR KEY

1 DECORATIVE RESOURCE TO BE USED IN THIS BOOK. In the previous chapter a summary of all the usual types of decoration was given.  In working harmony exercises, however, it is advisable to keep to the simplest types at first. Three types will be used in this book, viz. : (*a*) essential notes ; (*b*) unaccented passing notes ; (*c*) unaccented auxiliary notes of the mordent type.

2 TWO NOTES TO ONE.  The first stage is to discover the possibilities in two part harmony or counterpoint, when one part is moving twice as quickly as the other.  See Fig. 1. Notice that the alto is the bass.

**Fig. 1**

At present the accented notes of the quicker moving part must be essential.  The notes in between the accents must be one of the following :—

(*a*) *Another essential note belonging to the same chord.*

Fig. 2 (*a*) is correct ; (*b*) is incorrect ; (*c*) and (*d*) cannot be written at present, although the notes imply the tonic chord, because the second quaver makes a second inversion in each case, and second inversions are not yet known ; (*e*) also implies a second inversion ; ( *f* ) and (*g*) are satisfactory.

**Fig. 2**

Look through Fig. 1 and decide where essential notes occur, analysing the harmony at the same time.

(*b*) *An unaccented passing note.* See where these occur in Fig. 1. There are six.

(*c*) *An unaccented auxiliary note of the mordent or lower mordent type.* There are two in Fig. 1.

3 THE TYPE OF DECORATION TO USE. Suppose you have to decorate a plain part with notes twice as fast. The following decorations can be used, according to the interval between adjacent notes :—

(*a*) *Gap of a 3rd :* Passing note or chord note. See Fig. 3 (*a*).

(*b*) *Same note repeated :* Auxiliary note or chord note. See Fig. 3 (*b*).

(*c*) *Any other interval :* Chord note. See Fig. 3 (*c*) and (*d*).

**Fig. 3**

Use passing and auxiliary notes in preference to chord notes, as they produce a smoother flowing part. Opportunities for using auxiliary notes will, however, be rather rare.

4 FAULTY CONSECUTIVES. If faulty consecutives are
present in an original progression, adding a decoration does
not help matters. See Fig. 4 (*a*) and (*b*).

**Fig. 4**

On the other hand, decorations may cause a correct
passage to become incorrect. See Fig. 5 (*a*) and (*b*). When
using essential notes as decoration, it is well to avoid consecutive 5ths and 8ves on any part of adjacent beats. See
Fig. 5 (*c*). They can, however, be written if at least one note
is unessential and they are not next to each other. See
Fig. 5 (*d*).

**Fig. 5**

5 TREATMENT OF THE UNISON. A unison must be approached by contrary motion. See Fig. 6 (*a*). If it is
approached by similar motion, overlapping is produced.
See Fig. 6 (*b*). If it is approached by oblique motion the
effect is confused, and must be avoided. See Fig. 6 (*c*).

**Fig. 6**

**Exercise I.** Decorate either part (but not both) in the following exercises, so as to make a continuous half pulse movement, except at the cadences. Notice that the minim is the pulse in (*c*).

**Fig. 7**

leave undecorated

**Exercise II.** Add a part in pulse notes to the following exercises. Longer notes may be used at the cadences. Decide on the chord scheme before beginning to fill in, and take care that all accented notes in the quicker part belong to the chord you choose. Every note you write must be essential.

**Fig. 8**

*a)* **Add Alto**

15

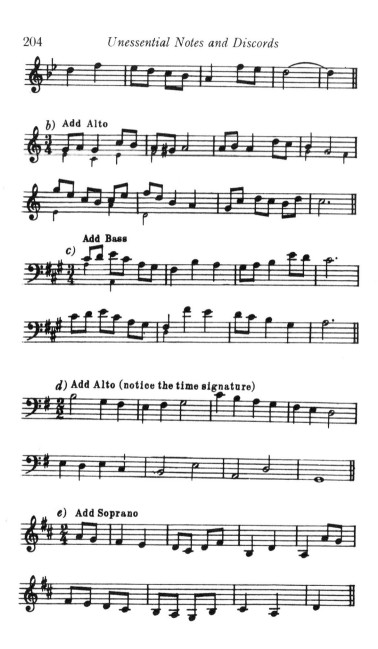

**Exercise 111.** Add a decorated part to the following exercises. Use half-pulse and pulse notes only, except for an occasional longer note at the cadences. Move by step as much as possible. Never have more than two notes to one of the given part. The instructions given in the Appendix can now be followed.

**Fig. 9**

Add Soprano in crotchets, with a dotted minim at each cadence

6 THREE AND FOUR NOTES TO ONE. Sometimes it happens that there are three or four notes to one. In such a case the first must be essential, and the second, third and fourth may be any of the following :—

(*a*) *Essential notes.* An essential note in any rhythmic position is free to leap, but use leaps sparingly. The Es in Fig. 10 (*a*), (*b*) and (*c*) are correctly treated each time, as they are essential and free to leap. A leap after step-wise movement is generally better taken in the opposite direction. Cf. Fig. 10 (*a*) and (*d*).

**Fig. 10**

(*b*) *Passing notes.* Use these as much as possible. But remember that they must continue in the same direction until they reach another essential note. Examine Fig. 11. In (*a*) the F, a passing note, is correctly treated ; in (*b*) it is incorrectly treated. But (*c*) is correct because the F is an essential note.

**Fig. 11**

(*c*) *Auxiliary notes.* Beware of overdoing these, particularly when there are three notes to one. Fig. 12 (*a*) is poor. As the third note of the mordent figure is a return to the essential note it is free to leap. Fig. 12 (*b*) and (*c*) are both correct.

7 TREATMENT OF ♩. ♪, ♩. ♪ and ♩. ♪♪     The added part must be essential against the dot. Fig. 13 (*a*) to (*d*) shows good treatment of these rhythms.

In (*a*) and (*b*) there is a long note against the dotted figure.

In (*c*) and (*d*) the added part moves to another essential note on the dot.

(*e*) and (*f*) are not quite so good, as the effect is jerky.     They may, however, be satisfactory in certain contexts.

(*g*) and (*h*) are wrong ; the F has been prematurely harmonised by the D.     At the moment of the dot the E is still heard and is the essential note to be harmonised.     The F is really a passing note.

Think of ♩. ♪ as ♩ ♫ (see (*i*) which is the same as (*g*)), ♩. ♪ as ♪♫ , and ♩. ♪♪ as ♪♫♫ , and you will then treat these figures correctly.

8 DECORATION IN TWO PARTS AT ONCE. This will be rare at present. It is possible under the following conditions :—

(a) If both notes are essential. See Fig. 14 (a).

(b) If both notes are unessential and (1) proceed in consecutive 3rds or 6ths or (2) sound an octave by contrary conjunct motion. See Fig. 14 (b), (c) and (d).

It is *not* possible at present under any other conditions. Do not attempt to combine an essential with an unessential note.

**Fig. 14**

9 MELODY RHYTHM. Both the given and the added part can now have a free rhythm, provided that it is musical and natural. A decorative part with a free varied rhythm is called " florid ". Remember the value of rhythmic contrast between two contrapuntal parts. It generally happens that when one part is moving quickly the other is moving slowly, and vice versa. Each has an interesting rhythm in turn. See Fig. 15.

**Fig. 15**

In florid writing it often happens that the movement is continuous except at the cadences. See Fig. 15. A sudden cessation may sound abrupt when once the movement has been established. Leave out the notes marked * in Fig. 15, in order to hear the effect. If the movement is only occasional this does not apply.

The entry of the added part is more clearly heard if it occurs after a rest. See Figs. 16 and 22.

**Fig. 16**

Remember also the value of imitation. See Figs. 15 and 21 (*b*). If the given part has a rest, at the beginning or elsewhere, the added part should move. When a rest occurs on a strong beat the added part, at that moment, must imply the same chord as that of the next note. See Fig. 17 (*a*). If it occurs on a weak beat then the chord implied must be the same as that of the previous note. See Fig. 17 (*b*).

**Fig. 17**

10 CHORD RHYTHM. Chords very rarely move more quickly than the beat. A quicker moving part will therefore be employing decoration. Cf. Fig. 18 (*a*) with the ungainly effect at (*b*).

**Fig. 18**

I  V  VI  Ib    IV  II  Vb  Ib  V  II  V        I

Chords often move less frequently than the beat, particularly in the cadence bar. Remember that the final cadence chord, at present, always occurs on an accent. Play Fig. 19, and choose chords for the cadence at the end of the first phrase.

**Fig. 19**

Then play the melody three times, harmonising the first cadence as at Fig. 20 (*a*), (*b*) and (*c*). The II*b* at the end of Fig. 20 (*c*) disturbs the phrasing, and sounds quite wrong.

**Fig. 20**

IIb    V        IIb    V___    IIb    V    IIb

Remember that chords often change only once a bar (see previous chapter).

A chord rhythm, once started, is often continued throughout an exercise. If it is disturbed it will probably be at or just before the cadence. The following are two good chord rhythm schemes :—

(a) $\frac{3}{4}$ I –V | VI—IV | II—V | I— — ‖

(b) $\frac{2}{4}$ I— | IV I$b$ | II— | V— | V— | I— | II$b$ V | I—‖

Fig. 21 shows workings of them.

**Fig. 21**

11 COMPOUND TIME. Exercises in $\frac{6}{8}$ time have, until this chapter, contained six beats in a bar. From now onwards they may contain only two, and you must decide how many there are before starting to work an exercise. Except in

very slow movements ⁶₈ is nearly always two beats in a bar. Fig. 22 shows two exercises in compound time. ⁹₈ and ¹²₈ would be treated similarly.

**Fig. 22**

**Exercise IV.** Add another florid part below the following melodies. Follow the method of working given in the appendix.

**Fig. 23**

**Exercise V.** Add a florid melody above the following basses :—

**Fig. 24**

SUMMARY OF RULES.

(1) Essential notes must occur on the accent (at present).

(2) Essential, passing, or auxiliary notes may occur in between the accents. Use passing and auxiliary notes in preference to essential notes, as they produce a smoother part.

(3) Decorations do not remedy faulty consecutives already present.

(4) Decorations should not produce consecutive 5ths or 8ves on any part of adjacent beats, unless at least one note is unessential, and they are not next to each other.

(5) Do not approach a unison by oblique motion.

(6) In dotted figures use an essential note against the dot.

(7) Two parts can only make decorations at the same time if (*a*) both are essential ; (*b*) both are unessential, and (1) proceed in consecutive 3rds or 6ths or (2) sound an 8ve by contrary conjunct motion.

(8) Aim for rhythmic contrast between the parts. Use occasional rests, and let the parts imitate each other.

(9) The chord rhythm must be recognised before an exercise is worked.

## CHAPTER III.

### DECORATED TWO PART WRITING, MINOR KEY

1 THE USE OF THE MELODIC MINOR. Decorated parts frequently move by step. But in the minor key trouble arises with step-wise movement, owing to the augmented 2nd between law and te, if the harmonic form of the scale is used. To avoid this the melodic minor may now be used for decorative purposes. It is important to realise however that, for the present, the notes of the melodic minor may only be used *unessentially and by step*. The harmonic minor must be used everywhere else. Fig. 1 (*a*) shows A♮ and B♭ correctly treated in C minor, as step wise unessential notes. 1 (*b*) shows them incorrectly treated, by leap, and as essential notes. Notice how vague the tonality feels in 1 (*b*). It is rather like E♭ major in bars 2 and 3, and C major in bars 5 and 6, yet there is no clear modulation to either key. The risk of unclear tonality is the main reason for the present restrictions.

**Fig. 1**

2 PASSING NOTES, MELODIC MINOR. There are four places where melodic minor passing notes can be used as decorations, filling in the gap between essential notes. They are as follows :—

(*a*) Soh rising to doh.  Soh lah te doh can be used.  See Fig. 2 (*a*).

(*b*) Doh falling to soh.  Doh taw law soh can be used.  See Fig 2 (*b*).

These idioms use the melodic minor in its scale-wise form, lah te being used ascending, and taw law descending.

(*c*) Soh to te, or te to soh.  Lah can be used.  See Fig. 2 (*c*) and (*d*).

(*d*) Doh to law or law to doh.  Taw can be used.  See Fig. 2 (*e*) and (*f*).

In these idioms the notes are *not* necessarily used as in the melodic minor ascending and descending scale.  Taw may be used ascending as well as descending, and lah descending as well as ascending.  It is the essential note that is the deciding factor.  Te used essentially requires lah used unessentially, in order to avoid the augmented interval te law.  Law used essentially requires taw, for the same reason.  Compare (*f*) and (*g*).

Fig. 2

3 AUXILIARY NOTES, MELODIC MINOR.  There are two places where these can be used.  They are as follows :—

(*a*) Law repeated.  Law taw law can be used.  See Fig. 3 (*a*).

(*b*) Te repeated.  Te lah te can be used.  See Fig. 3 (*b*).

Here again it is not a question of ascending or descending scale.  The essential note is decorated with the unessential note which does not produce an augmented interval.  Compare (*b*) and (*c*).

**Fig. 3**

If you remember that the essential note must always belong to the harmonic minor and that the augmented 2nd cannot be used, you will use these idioms correctly.

**Exercise I.** Decorate the following exercises in either or both parts, as you think fit, making use of melodic minor notes where possible.

**Fig. 4**

**Exercise II.** Add another melodic part to the following exercises. Notes must not move more quickly than the pulse and every note must be essential—which means that *you* cannot use the melodic minor, although the given part does so.

**Fig. 5**

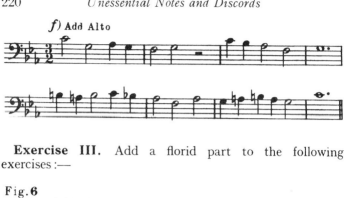

**Exercise III.** Add a florid part to the following exercises :—

SUMMARY OF RULES.

The following idioms employing the melodic minor can be used :—

(1) *Soh* lah te *doh*     ⎱ Two passing notes between essen-
(2) *Doh* taw law *soh* ⎰ tial notes.
(3) *Soh* lah *te*, and *te* lah *soh*   ⎱ One passing note be-
(4) *Doh* taw *law* and *law* taw *doh* ⎰ tween essential notes.
(5) *Law* taw *law* ⎱ Auxiliary note between essential notes.
(6) *Te* lah *te*    ⎰

The essential notes are in italics.

# CHAPTER IV.

## DECORATED FOUR PART WRITING

1 DECORATION IN ONE PART AT A TIME. In simple harmony exercises the most usual decoration is an occasional half pulse note between the beats. This is sometimes a harmony note, sometimes an auxiliary note, but most commonly a passing note. When harmony notes are a third away from each other it is generally possible to insert a passing note in any of the four parts. But do not alter a given part unless told to do so. Fig. 1 (*b*) shows a more interesting version of Fig. 1 (*a*).

Fig. 1

2 DECORATION IN TWO PARTS AT ONCE. As in two part writing, this can only occur if (*a*) both notes are essential; or (*b*) both notes are unessential and (1) make consecutive 3rds or 6ths, or (2) take the same note by contrary conjunct motion. Fig. 2 (*a*) shows a decorated form of Fig. 1 (*a*), with decorations in two parts at once. Analyse it.

Fig. 2

Fig. 2 (*b*) shows the second bar incorrectly treated.

Two decorations occurring at the same time *must* at present have the same rhythm—both ♩ ♩ ♩, ♫ ♩ ♩, ♩ ♪ ♩ or ♩. ♪ ♩ *etc.* Fig. 2 (*c*) shows bar 3 of Fig. 2 (*a*) with decorations in two different rhythms. This is a much more advanced technique, and should not be attempted at present.

Decorations must not be written in more than two parts at once at this stage.

3 DOTTED FIGURES. Be careful about the treatment of dotted figures. If all the parts move in the same rhythm, as at Fig. 3 (*a*), the effect is even more jerky than it was in two parts. (*b*) is incorrect, (*c*) to (*f*) are correct. Analyse them, referring to Part IV, Chapter II, para. 7, if necessary.

**Fig. 8**

4 CONSECUTIVES. Remember that decorations do not remove the effect of faulty consecutives, and may produce fresh ones. There is more need for care when four parts are concerned. In correcting the movement between chords 1 and 2 in Fig. 4 (*a*), both the F and the E in the soprano have to be checked in relation to all the other parts.

**Fig. 4**

Harmony notes used as decoration are dangerous from the consecutive point of view. In Fig. 4 (*b*) both the G and the B in the soprano have to be considered ; so it is almost like writing five part harmony. A very good solution of this difficulty is to let another part have the same notes in the opposite order, as at (*c*). Consecutives are then avoided, and the doubling remains the same. Another alternative is to move the tenor to a different harmony note, as at (*d*), but this requires even more careful checking, as both notes in the soprano and tenor may cause trouble with the other parts.

5 FIGURED BASS. When a figured bass is given, decorations are generally indicated by figures, as in Fig. 5 (*a*) If the decoration is in the bass, a line is used to indicate that the chord is unchanged, as in Fig. 5 (*b*).

**Fig. 5**

6 MAJOR AND MINOR KEY. From now onwards the major and minor key will not be treated separately. The directions given will apply to both, unless the contrary is stated. Before starting to work an exercise be sure that you realise whether it is in a major or minor key.

**Exercise I.** Decorate any of the four parts in the following examples as you think fit. Use passing notes mainly. Give two versions of (*b*).

**Fig. 6**

**Exercise II.** Add parts for A.T.B. to the following melodies, introducing occasional decoration, mainly by means of passing notes. Think out the chord rhythm and decide which melody notes are best treated as unessential. In Fig. 7 (*a*) the chord rhythm is mostly ♩ ♩ ‖. The chords move in crotchet rhythm in (*b*), and in dotted crotchet rhythm in (*c*).

**Fig. 7**

**Exercise III.** Add parts for S.A.T. to the following basses :—

Fig. 8

**Exercise IV.** Add parts for S.A.T. to the following figured basses :—

Fig. 9

EAR TESTS. In a four part harmony ear test the average pupil at this stage cannot be expected to hear more than the melody and bass and the changes of harmony. The movement of individual parts should not be asked for. But the teacher may, if he wishes, give some very simple dictation tests including decorations.

SUMMARY OF RULES.

(1) Two decorations occurring at the same time must have the same rhythm (at present).

(2) Decorations must not be written in more than two parts at once (at present).

(3) Decorations over a figured bass are generally indicated by figures. A line under moving bass notes indicates that the chord is unchanged.

## CHAPTER V.

### SECOND INVERSIONS. Ic AND IVc CADENTIAL; Ic AND Vc PASSING

It is assumed that paras. 11–13 of Part I, Chapter III have previously been studied.

1 DISCORDS. A discord is a combination of sounds which is incomplete and requires a resolution. It sometimes requires a preparation also.

You have been using discords as unessential notes in this section of the book. Now they are to be used as essential notes of the chord.

2 SECOND INVERSIONS. All triads in their second inversions, *i.e.*, all $^6_4$ chords, are discords. This is a little surprising, for they consist of the same notes as their root positions and first inversions. But there is a great difference in sound, owing to the presence of the discordant 4th *with the bass*. Compare the effect of the first three chords in Fig. 1, and play the examples in paras. 11–13 of Part I, Chapter III.

**Fig.1**

I    Ib    Ic

In this chapter, only the primary triads will be used in their second inversion. And even they will only be used under certain definite conditions. Do not think of $^6_4$ chords as additions to the vocabulary, to be used as freely as, *e.g.*, II*b*. They occur frequently, but only in certain definite places. At present they must not be used except as stated in this chapter.

3 $^6_4$ CHORDS AS DECORATIONS. There are two kinds of decoration, melodic and harmonic. You have already learnt how chords can be decorated melodically. Complete chords can also be used to decorate the main chord progression, and thus make harmonic decoration. The $^6_4$ chord is a decorative chord, and it should always be thought of in this way. The next paragraphs show some of its decorative uses.

4 V DECORATED BY A $^6_4$ CHORD. Fig. 2 (*a*) shows a cadence ending with V. (*b*) shows a decorated version of it. The E and C in soprano and alto have been held over as suspensions and the suspensions have produced a new chord, I*c*. The unessential notes have become essential. Similarly compare (*c*) and (*d*). This time, accented passing notes have produced I*c*. At (*e*) the chord has been produced by a suspension and an accented passing note. It should be clear that in all these cases I*c* is a decoration of V.

**Fig. 2**

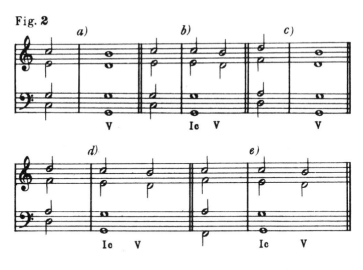

Fig. 2 shows how I*c* first came to be used. It was not thought of as being a chord, it was considered to be a combination of unessential notes. Nowadays it has become essential, and we do not feel that it must be prepared by particular notes, as in Fig. 2. But we still feel that it requires to resolve on to V, and that it is a decoration of V.

5 Ic V. In any cadence using V, *i.e.*, Perfect, Imperfect or Interrupted, Ic can be put in the place of V and resolve on to V afterwards. It is important to realise that this means it must always come on a stronger accent than V. Ic creates stress, V is the resolution of that stress. Fig. 3 shows a number of cadences containing V. Fig. 4 shows the same cadences with Ic decorating V in every case. Compare these examples, analysing the harmony carefully, and naming the cadences made.

Fig. 3

Fig. 4

In Fig. 4 (*b*) Ic comes on the 2nd beat, and V on the 3rd. This is quite satisfactory. Ic V still has the effect of being —∪. But V must on no account come on a stronger beat than Ic. Play Fig. 4 as if the bar lines came between Ic and V, in order to hear the halting effect. In one chord a bar rhythm, Ic and V may have a bar each.

6 IVc I. I in a perfect or plagal cadence is occasionally decorated by IVc in a similar manner. Compare Figs. 5 and 6.

**Fig. 5**

**Fig. 6**

7 CADENTIAL $^6_4$s.  The $^6_4$ chords described in paras. 5 and 6 are called " cadential $^6_4$s ".  V$c$ is not used cadentially, as it would resolve on II, which is not a cadence chord.

8 DOUBLING.  In four part writing the bass note (*i.e.*, the 5th) of *all* $^6_4$ chords is doubled, and the root and 3rd are each used once.  Analyse the doubling in Figs. 4 and 6 and compare it with Fig. 7.

**Fig. 7**

All Bad

9 MELODIC PROGRESSION.   In cadential $^6_4$s the bass note, the 5th, stays to become the root of the chord upon which it resolves.  The doubled 5th generally remains as a binding note, and the other two notes move down by step.  Analyse

the movement in Figs. 4 and 6. Occasionally, however, the upper parts do not move in this way. Provided that the ⁶₄ resolves on to a root position on the same bass note, and the doubling is correct in each chord, the upper parts are free. See Fig. 8.

**Fig. 8**

10 THE APPROACH TO A CADENTIAL ⁶₄. As Ic is merely a decoration of V it will be realised that any chord which can precede V can precede Ic. Analyse the chord choice in Figs. 2, 3 and 4.

Notice that I and Ib can be used before Ic, in spite of the accent being ∪—, because Ib | Ic V ‖ is really Ib | V ‖ , decorated. V and Vb are the chords which must not be used before Ic V.

In future, when choosing cadence chords, always see if Ic can be used before V, when V is on a weak beat, and then choose an appropriate chord before Ic.

IVc I, used cadentially, can only be preceded by chords which can come before I at a cadence, *i.e.*, IV and V and their inversions, and VIIb.

11 MASCULINE AND FEMININE ENDINGS. A cadence is said to have a masculine ending if its last chord comes on a strong beat, and a feminine ending if the last chord comes on a weak beat. Until this chapter, all your cadence endings have been masculine. But Ic V in place of V at an imperfect cadence and IVc I in place of I at a perfect or plagal cadence turn masculine into feminine endings. Play through Figs. 2–6, deciding which cadences have feminine endings, and comparing their effect with the stronger, but less graceful, masculine ones.

A phrase ending on a weak beat always implies decoration of some kind. It may be melodic only, in which case the

chord must come on the strong beat as in Fig. 9 (*a*) and (*b*).
Or it may be harmonic, in which case a cadential $^6_4$ is probably
required, as in (*c*).

**Fig. 9**

12 FIGURED BASS. A second inversion is indicated by the
figures $^6_4$. When it is followed by a root position on the
same bass note, as in the cadential $^6_4$, the figures $^5_3$ are written
to indicate the change of chord. See Fig. 9 (*c*).

CHORD SINGING.

**Fig. 10**

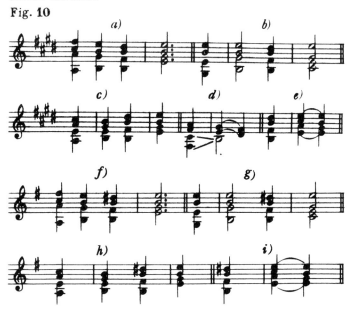

EAR TESTS. The examples in Fig. 11 can also be given in the tonic minor except (*e*).

**Fig. 11**

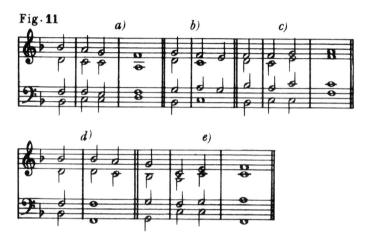

**Exercise I.** Change the following masculine endings into feminine ones, by adding cadential $^6_4$s. Work backwards from the last chord. Repeat the doubled bass note and move the other notes up by step, so that they may fall by step. Then check, to see that you have produced the right chord.

**Fig. 12**

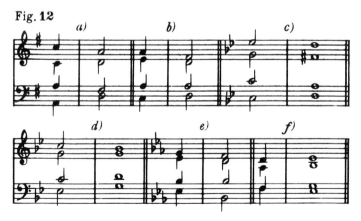

17

**Exercise II.** Harmonise these cadences, using a cadential $^6_4$ in each case :—

Fig. **13**

**Exercise III.** Write the following cadences, using a cadential $^6_4$ in each case, preceded by one other chord : (*a*) perfect in G major ; (*b*) imperfect in D minor ; (*c*) interrupted in B♭ major ; (*d*) imperfect in A♭ major ; (*e*) perfect in E minor.

13 THE PASSING $^6_4$.   A $^6_4$ can also be used as a decorating chord on a weak beat, between two positions of the same chord.   Compare the examples in Figs. 14 and 15.   In Fig. 15 (*a*) a passing note in the treble, a passing note in the bass, and an auxiliary note in the tenor, together produce a new chord, V*c*, on the second beat.   As it has the effect of a passing chord it is called a passing $^6_4$.   (*b*), (*c*) and (*d*) are treated similarly.   Play Figs. 14 and 15 in C minor also.

Fig. **14**

**Fig. 15**

14 USES OF THE PASSING $^6_4$. At present, the passing $^6_4$ must only occur when the melody is moving doh ray me, me ray doh, fah soh lah, or lah soh fah (and the equivalent in the minor key), and the bass is taking the same notes in the reverse order, as in Fig. 15. V*c* occurs between I and I*b*, and I*c* occurs between IV and IV*b*. IV*c* cannot be used in this way at present, as it would have to come between VII*b* and VII, and VII being a diminished triad, cannot be used.

The passing $^6_4$ chord must give the effect of passing to and from the main harmonies, and must therefore come on a weak beat.

I, V*c*, I*b* is almost identical with I, VII*b*, I*b*. Play Fig. 16 and compare their sound. VII*b* is a little softer and is generally preferable.

**Fig. 16**

15 CONSECUTIVE 2nd INVERSIONS. These may appear in one progression, as a kind of double decoration. I*b* | I ‖ (see Fig. 17 (*a*)) can be decorated by a passing $^6_4$, thus making the progression I*b* V*c* | I ‖ (see (*b*)). The I can be further decorated by a cadential $^6_4$, thus making I*b* V*c* | IV*c* I ‖ (see (*c*)).

**Fig. 17**

16 CONSECUTIVE 4THS. In using the progression mentioned in paragraph 15, consecutive perfect 4ths *with the
bass* may be produced, as in Fig. 17 (*d*). These sound as crude
as consecutive perfect 5ths, and must be avoided. They can
only occur in this particular progression, at present, however, and they will not occur even then, if the parts move
naturally and smoothly. They are, of course, satisfactory
in upper parts.

17 DECORATION OF $^6_4$ CHORDS. As $^6_4$ chords are themselves
decorations, and as the parts move mostly by step or have
binding notes, it is not often possible or advisable to add
further melodic decoration. This is particularly true of the
passing $^6_4$.

CHORD SINGING.

**Fig. 18**

EAR TESTS.

**Fig. 19**

**Exercise IV.** Add passing ⁶₄s to the following progressions :—

**Fig. 20**

**Exercise V.** Harmonise the following progressions, using a passing ⁶₄ in each case :—

**Fig. 21**

Vc    IVc    I

NOTE.—From now to the end of the book, exercises both without and with melodic decoration are included. Those with decoration can be omitted if desired.

**Exercise VI.**  Harmonise the following melodies :—

Fig. 22

**Exercise VII.** Harmonise the following figured basses :—

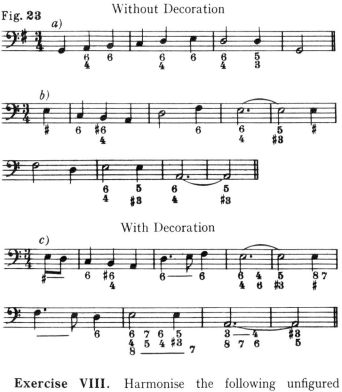

Fig. 23     Without Decoration

**Exercise VIII.** Harmonise the following unfigured basses :—

Fig. 24     Without Decoration

## With Decoration

SUMMARY OF RULES AND CHORD PROGRESSIONS.

(1) All 2nd inversions are discords, and must only be used under special conditions.

(2) 2nd inversions are decorative chords.

(3) A cadential $^6_4$ resolves on to a root position on the same bass note. The progressions which can be used thus are I*c* V and IV*c* I.

(4) A cadential $^6_4$ must occur on a stronger accent than its resolution.

(5) In four part writing, the bass note, *i.e.*, the 5th, of *all* $^6_4$ chords is doubled, and the root and 3rd are each used once.

(6) In deciding what chords can be used before a cadential $^6_4$, imagine the progression without the $^6_4$.

(7) The use of cadential $^6_4$s sometimes creates feminine endings.

(8) A second inversion is figured $^6_4$. When a root position on the same bass note follows it is figured $^5_3$.

(9) A passing $^6_4$ can occur when the melody is d r m, m r d, f s l or l s f (and the equivalent in the minor key) and the bass has the same notes in the reverse order.

(10) A passing $^6_4$ occurs on a weak accent.

(11) Consecutive 2nd inversions can occur in the progression I*b* V*c* | IV*c* I ‖ , and in no other.

(12) Avoid consecutive perfect 4ths with the bass.

## CHAPTER VI.

## THE DOMINANT 7th, RESOLVING ON TO I, Ib AND VI

It is assumed that para. 14 of Part 1, Chapter III, has previously been studied.

1 SEVENTHS. Every diatonic triad can have a diatonic 7th added to it, and in each case a discord is produced. Some of the chords are more discordant than others. Play Fig. 1.

**Fig. 1**

2 THE DOMINANT 7TH. Of these sevenths, that on the dominant is unique, as it is the only one consisting of a major triad and a minor 7th. It has a soft and pleasing effect, and is much more frequently used than any of the other 7ths.

It consists of the same notes in the major and minor key. See Fig. 2. There are two discordant intervals, the minor 7th formed by the root and 7th, soh and fah, and the diminished 5th formed by the 3rd and 7th, te and fah. They sound satisfactory if the fah falls to me (maw in the minor key) and the te rises to doh, as in Fig. 2.

**Fig. 2**

3 HIGHER DISCORDS ON V. It will interest you to know that it is possible to continue adding 3rds to V, and thus to produce dominant 9ths, 11ths and 13ths, as at Fig. 3 (a),

(*b*) and (*c*). The addition of yet another 3rd, as at (*d*), would bring you back to the root.

Fig. 3

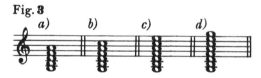

These chords are of frequent occurrence, particularly at cadences, and you should be able to recognise them. Obviously some of the notes will have to be left out, in four part harmony.

Fig. 4 shows some examples. Play and analyse them. The highest discord is usually in the melody.

Fig. 4

4 $^7$V PRODUCED BY UNESSENTIAL NOTES. Like the $^6_4$ chord, $^7$V was first used unessentially. Fig. 5 (*a*) to (*d*) shows it produced by passing notes. (*e*) shows $^7$V and $^7$II produced by suspensions.

Fig. 5

As its sound became more familiar it gradually began to be treated as an essential chord, and nowadays there is no need to prepare it. But fah and te still require resolution, so ⁷V usually resolves on to a triad containing doh and me (or maw), *i.e.*, I or VI.

**5** RESOLUTION OF ⁷V. As the chapter heading indicates, we are now concerned with the resolutions on to I, I*b* or VI, which are by far the most common. Fig. 6 (*a*) and (*b*) show ⁷V resolving on to I and VI. (Notice that the 3rd is doubled in VI, as in the progression V VI.) The root position of ⁷V does not resolve on to I*b* (see (*c*)), as it produces an ugly doubled 3rd.

**Fig. 6**

**6** RESOLUTIONS OF INVERSIONS OF ⁷V. Write out the inversions for yourself and resolve them. You will discover the following :—

(1) ⁷V*b* must resolve on to I, owing to the presence of te in the bass. See Fig. 7 (*a*).

(2) ⁷V*c* also moves to I. As the chord is a 2nd inversion, the bass should not leap, so the chord cannot move to VI, and movement to I*b* would produce a doubled 3rd. See (*b*) and (*c*).

(3) ⁷V*d* must move to I*b*, owing to the presence of fah in the bass. See (*d*).

**Fig. 7**

You will realise, therefore, that only the root position can resolve on to VI, and only the last inversion can resolve on to I*b*.

7 OMITTING AND DOUBLING NOTES. As there are four notes in the chord, there is generally one of each, in four part harmony. If the root or 7th is omitted the chord is no longer ⁷V. It is more possible to omit the 3rd than in a triad, as the 7th softens the effect (see Fig. 8 (*a*)), but we rarely do so. The 5th can be omitted. See (*b*).

**Fig. 8**

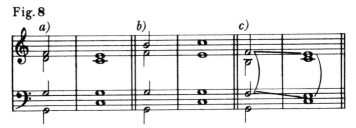

The 3rd and 7th cannot be doubled, as they are discords, and consecutive 8ves would be produced when they were resolved. See Fig. 8 (*c*). So when the 5th is omitted the root is usually doubled, as at (*b*). In the inversions the chord is always complete, and soh acts as a binding note. See Fig. 7 (*a*), (*b*) and (*d*).

8 HARMONIC PROGRESSION. Do not let the root and 7th move to or from an 8ve by similar motion. The effect is ugly. See Fig. 9.

**Fig. 9**

CHORD SINGING. Fig. 10 can also be sung in the tonic minor, by changing the signature to one flat, and adding sharps to all the Cs.

**Fig. 10**

EAR TESTS. The examples in Fig. 11 can also be given in F minor. Tell the pupil to decide which voices have fah and te.

**Fig. 11**

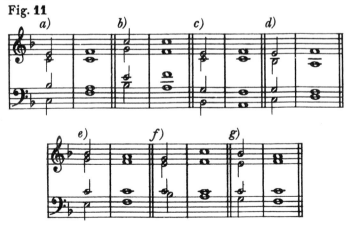

**Exercise I.** Resolve the following chords. Resolve te and fah first, then move the other notes.

**Fig. 12**

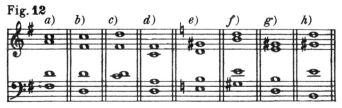

**Exercise II.** Precede the following chords with a dominant 7th. Place te and fah where they can resolve correctly, before adding the other notes

**Fig. 13**

**Exercise III.** Harmonise the following fragments, using ⁷V, either in root position or inverted, as the first chord in each case.

**Fig. 14**

9 IRREGULAR RESOLUTION OF ⁷V*c*. ⁷V*c* can resolve on to
I*b* if fah rises to soh, thus avoiding the doubled 3rd, and this
irregular resolution is very common. See Fig. 15 (*a*). Me
fah soh is frequently harmonised in this way. The progression backwards, soh fah me, is also very common. In this
case the resolution is normal. See (*b*).

**Fig. 15**

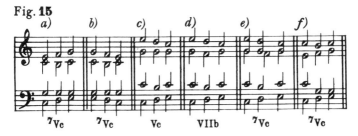

Compare VII*b*, V*c*, and ⁷V*c*. You will realise that ⁷V*c* is
VII*b* and V*c* added together. The chords sound very much
alike, and are used in similar positions. They all have a
" passing " effect. Cf. all the examples in Fig. 15. (*e*) is
in five part harmony, and you cannot therefore use it yet.
Notice that all the examples in Fig. 15 have the same bass.
Play them in C minor also.

10 ORNAMENTAL RESOLUTIONS. ⁷V can be decorated
before resolving, and this may mean the disappearance of
fah or te. But these notes must eventually resolve. See
Fig. 16.

**Fig. 16**

11 TWO POSITIONS OF ⁷V. When ⁷V is repeated, fah and
te obviously cannot resolve immediately. They must

resolve from their last position, and the part that had the first fah must fall. See Fig. 17 (*a*) and (*b*).

**Fig. 17**

CHORD SINGING. Sing Fig. 18 in B♭ minor also.

**Fig. 18**

**Exercise IV.** Harmonise the following fragments, using ⁷V, either in root position or inverted, at least once in each case.

**Fig. 19**

12 USES OF ⁷V. Generally speaking, ⁷V can be used where V would be good, providing that it is possible to resolve it correctly in the next chord.

$^7$V can be used in place of V.  See Fig. 20 (*a*) and (*b*)
$^7$V*b* can be used in place of V*b*.  See Fig. 20 (*c*) and (*d*).
$^7$V*c* can be used in place of V*c* or VII*b*.  See Fig. **15**.
$^7$V*d* can be used in place of V.  See Fig. 20 (*e*) and (*f*).

**Fig. 20**

Notice that, in addition to soh, te and ray, a fah in the melody or the bass can be harmonised by $^7$V if it can resolve correctly.

**13** APPROACH TO $^7$V.  Any chord that leads well to V is also good before $^7$V.  See Fig. 21.

**Fig. 21**

14 APPROACH TO INVERSIONS OF ⁷V. Think of the inversions of ⁷V as explained in para. 12, and you will use them correctly. They are frequently used between two positions of the tonic chord. See Fig. 22.

**Fig. 22**

15 I*c* ⁷V, AND I*c* ⁷V*d*. I*c* can resolve on to the dominant 7th. Either of the sohs may move to fah. Fig. 23 (*a*) and (*b*) show a soh in an upper part doing this, and I*c* resolving on to ⁷V. If the bass note moves down, then I*c* resolves on to ⁷V*d* as at (*c*). Remember this latter progression, it is a useful way of inverting a cadence.

**Fig. 23**

16 THE SAME BASS NOTE ∪—. The same bass note may be used ∪— if the second note is the 7th of a new chord, as it sounds sufficiently discordant to create a new effect. See Fig. 24.

**Fig. 24**

**17** FIGURED BASS. Fig. 25 illustrates the figuring used for a chord of the 7th and its inversions. The figures in brackets are generally implied. Notice that the figures which *must* be present are those that show the presence of both the root and the 7th.

**Fig. 25**

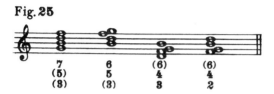

CHORD SINGING. Sing the examples in Fig. 26 in the tonic minor also.

**Fig. 26**

EAR TESTS. Progressions similar to those illustrated in paras. 9–16 should be given.

**Exercise V.** Harmonise the following fragments, using $^7$V, either in root position or inverted, at least once in each case.

**Fig. 27**

18 ⁷V AT CADENCES. ⁷V is frequently used in place of V at perfect and interrupted cadences. See Fig. 6 (*a*) and (*b*). But do not use ⁷V for the final chord at an imperfect cadence, as it is too unfinished. It is very common, however, for a phrase to end with V, and for fah to be added immediately afterwards, as a link to the next phrase. When this is done in the bass, ⁷V*d* is produced. See Fig. 28.

**Fig. 28**

Like V I*b*, V*b* I and V VI, the inversions of ⁷V are most helpful when a finished cadence is to be avoided. See Fig. 29.

**Fig. 29**

19 ⁷V AT BEGINNINGS OF PHRASES. Fig. 30 shows some common beginnings of phrases.

**Fig. 30**

20 ⁷V IN THE MIDDLE OF PHRASES. The inversions of ⁷V are very common in the middle of a phrase, particularly between two positions of the tonic chord. Look out for chances to use them, and remember that fah can be harmonised by ⁷V. Analyse the chords in Fig. 31.

**Fig. 31**

**Exercise VI.** Write the following cadences, using three chords in each. Every progression must include a dominant 7th. (*a*) Perfect in E major ; (*b*) interrupted in A minor ; (*c*) inverted perfect in B♭ major ; (*d*) interrupted in E♭ major ; (*e*) inverted perfect in G minor.

**Exercise VII.** Harmonise the following melodies :—

Without Decoration

**Fig. 32**

With Decoration

Without Decoration

**Exercise VIII.** Harmonise the following figured and unfigured basses :—

## With Decoration

SUMMARY OF RULES AND CHORD PROGRESSIONS.

(1) In $^7$V fah normally falls to me (or maw) and te rises to doh. Fah rises, however, in moving from $^7$Vc to 1b.

(2) The resolutions of $^7$V are as follows : $^7$V to I or VI ; $^7$Vb to I ; $^7$Vc to I or Ib (irregular resolution) ; $^7$Vd to Ib.

(3) In four part harmony $^7$V generally contains every note once, but occasionally the 5th is omitted, and the root doubled. It is possible to omit the 3rd.

(4) Do not let the root and 7th move to or from an 8ve by similar motion.

(5) $^7$V$c$ is used as a passing chord between I and I$b$, particularly when the melody is me fah soh, or soh fah me (and the equivalent in the minor key).

(6) $^7$V can be resolved ornamentally.

(7) When $^7$V moves from one position to another the last position must resolve correctly.

(8) $^7$V can be used in place of V.
   $^7$V$b$ can be used in place of V$b$.
   $^7$V$c$ can be used in place of V$c$ or VII$b$.
   $^7$V$d$ can be used in place of V.

(9) I$c$ can resolve on to $^7$V and $^7$V$d$, at a cadence.

(10) The same bass note can be used $\cup$— if the second note is the 7th of a new chord.

(11) Figured bass :—

$$^7V = \begin{Bmatrix} 7 \\ (5) \\ (3) \end{Bmatrix} ; \quad {}^7Vb = \begin{Bmatrix} 6 \\ 5 \\ (3) \end{Bmatrix} ; \quad {}^7Vc = \begin{Bmatrix} (6) \\ 4 \\ 3 \end{Bmatrix} ; \quad {}^7Vd = \begin{Bmatrix} (6) \\ 4 \\ 2 \end{Bmatrix}$$

(12) $^7$V and its inversions are frequently used at the beginning, middle, and ends of phrases. Remember that fah can be harmonised by this chord, as well as soh, te and ray.

## CHAPTER VII.

## SECOND INVERSIONS AND DOMINANT 7ths IN TWO PART WRITING

1 THE CADENTIAL ⁶₄. This can now be implied in two part writing. See Fig. 1. At (*b*) and (*c*) an essential discord is used for the first time in two part work.

**Fig. 1**

2 THE PASSING ⁶₄. See Fig. 2. The Ds in (*a*) and the Gs in (*b*) can be thought of as implied passing ⁶₄s, or as simple passing notes.

**Fig. 2**

3 THE DOMINANT 7TH. This is frequently implied in two part writing. See Fig. 3. The discords of the augmented 4th with its inversion the diminished 5th, and the minor 7th with its inversion the major 2nd, can all be used, providing that they resolve correctly. It is very common to imply two positions of ⁷V, as at (*h*), (*i*) and (*j*).

**Fig. 3**

CHORD SINGING. Figs 1, 2 and 3 should be sung as well as played.

EAR TESTS.

**Fig. 4**

**Exercise I.** Add interesting melodies below the following :—

Without Decoration

**Fig. 5**

a) Add Alto

b) Add Bass

With Decoration

c) Add Alto

**Exercise II.** Add interesting melodies above the following :—

### Without Decoration

**Fig. 6**

### With Decoration

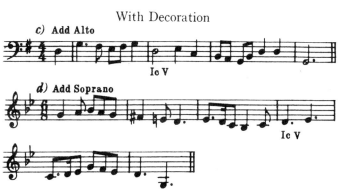

There are no new rules.

# PART V

# LESS USUAL CHORDS AND PROGRESSIONS, AND MODULATION

## CHAPTER I.

### THE ESSENTIAL USE OF THE MELODIC MINOR

1 LAH AND TAW USED ESSENTIALLY. Thus far you have not been able to use the 6th and 7th degrees of the scale next to each other, as essential notes, in the minor key, owing to the augmented 2nd between law and te. You have used lah and taw of the melodic minor for unessential notes, to get out of this difficulty. Now these notes are to be used essentially.

When lah and taw are used unessentially, several melodic progressions are possible. (See Part IV, Chapter III.) But when used essentially the melodic part concerned *must* follow the melodic minor scale, *i.e.*, the 6th and 7th degrees rising must be lah te, and falling, must be taw law. See Fig. 1 (*a*) and (*b*). In practice, the part usually follows the scale line between soh and doh, *i.e.*, soh lah te doh and doh taw law soh. See Fig. 1 (*c*) and (*d*). Doh lah te doh is fairly frequent however, and soh taw law soh is occasionally found. See (*e*) and (*f*).

**Fig. 1**    *a)*    *b)*    *c)*    *d)*    *e)*    *f)*

The important points to realise are :—

(1) The melodic minor is only used if the 6th and 7th degrees occur *together*.

(2) Lah must be used ascending to te ;

Taw must be used descending to law.

2 RESULTING ALTERATION OF TRIADS. Some queer things happen to triads as a result of these alterations.

Lah turns VI from a major into a diminished triad. See Fig. 2 (*a*).

Lah turns IV from a minor into a major triad. See Fig. 2 (*b*).

Lah turns II from a diminished into a minor triad. See Fig. 2 (*c*).

Taw turns VII from a diminished into a major triad. See Fig. 2 (*d*).

Taw turns V from a major into a minor triad. See Fig. 2 (*e*).

Taw turns III from an augmented into a major triad. See Fig. 2 (*f*).

3 CHORD CHOICE. Instead of trying to learn the above list of alterations and memorising lists of progressions, remember the three following points :—

(*a*) If the alteration turns a discord into a concord the chord can be used ; if it turns a concord into a discord it is wiser not to use the chord.

e.g., in using lah avoid VI (Fig. 2 (*a*), but use II (Fig. 2 (*c*)).

(*b*) With the above proviso, follow the ordinary principles of chord choice.

(*c*) Consecutive 1st inversions are frequently used, particularly when a part moves taw law soh.

Fig. 3 shows some common progressions using lah, and Fig. 4 shows some using taw. Analyse them carefully, and notice the frequent use of consecutive 1st inversions.

Fig. 4

Progressions using the melodic minor can easily sound unnatural. It is most important to *hear* what you have written.

4 DOUBLING. It is not generally wise to double lah. Taw can be doubled if one part is following the scale line, as in Fig. 1. Analyse the doublings in Figs. 3 and 4.

5 USE OF TAW. If not carefully managed, taw gives the impression of a modulation to the relative major. To avoid this, use te in the next chord but one. See Fig. 4.

**Exercise I.** Add one chord before and two chords after each of the following chords. Fill in the part using the melodic minor first.

**Fig. 5**

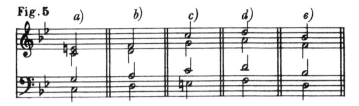

**Exercise II.** Add A.T.B. to the following melodies :—

Without Decoration.

**Fig. 6** *a)*

*b)*

V IVb Vb

**Exercise III.** Add S.A.T. to the following figured and unfigured basses :—

Without Decoration.

**Fig. 7** *a)*

*b)*

**Exercise IV.** Add interesting melodies below the following :—

Without Decoration.

With Decoration.

**Exercise V.** Add interesting melodies above the following :—

Without Decoration.

With Decoration.

SUMMARY OF RULES AND CHORD PROGRESSIONS.

(1) The melodic minor is used essentially when a melodic part moves lah te or taw law.

(2) Use any concords which result from the melodic minor and which form good progressions.

(3) Consecutive 1st inversions employing the melodic minor are common.

(4) Do not double lah. Taw can be doubled if one part is following the scale line.

(5) Use te in the next chord but one after taw.

## CHAPTER II.

## III AND IIIb MAJOR KEY. DIMINISHED AND AUGMENTED TRIADS

1 RARELY USED CHORDS. This chapter is concerned with all the diatonic triads, root position or first inversion, which you have not yet used, viz. :—

(a) III and IIIb, major key, root position and 1st inversion of a minor triad. Concords.

(b) III and IIIb, minor key, root position and 1st inversion of an augmented triad. Discords.

(c) VII major key, and II and VII, minor key, root positions of diminished triads. Discords.

It is wise to think of them as quite exceptional, and only to use them under the conditions stated here.

2 SEQUENCES. Any of the chords mentioned in this chapter may be used freely in the course of a sequence. Harmonic sequences frequently consist of two chords, whose roots are a 4th apart, repeated at a higher or lower pitch. The first two chords are usually common ones, and the rare chords occur in the repetitions. Analyse Fig. 1 (a) and (b).

3 CONSECUTIVE 1ST INVERSIONS. Unusual chords sound satisfactory in a series of 1st inversions with the root at the top. Analyse Fig. 2 (a) and (b).

19

Fig.2 a)          b)

4 OTHER USES OF III AND III*b*, MAJOR KEY.

(*a*) I III IV I.  When the Melody moves doh te lah soh.
See Fig. 3 (*a*).

(*b*) V III (or III*b*) VI.  III is used after V, whose " auxiliary " it is, and resolves on to a chord whose root is
a 4th above, *i.e.*, the strongest root progression.  See
(*b*) and (*c*).

(*c*) III*b* with the root at the top is used in place of V in a
perfect or interrupted cadence.  Compare with [13]V,
mentioned in Part IV, Chapter VI, para. 3.  The bass
note must be doubled.  The exposed 8ves are satisfactory here.  See (*d*) and (*e*).

Fig.3 *a)*          *b)*

**Exercise I.** Harmonise the following fragments, in the major key, using III or III*b* once in each :—

5 OTHER USES OF DIMINISHED AND AUGMENTED TRIADS. In addition to the progressions described in paras. 2 and 3 these chords can be used as stated in paras. 6, 7 and 8.

6 THE 5TH IN THE ROOT POSITION OF DIMINISHED AND AUGMENTED TRIADS. This note is apt to sound so discordant that it is as well both to prepare and resolve it, unless it occurs in a sequence. It is prepared by being sounded in the same voice in the previous chord. See Fig. 5. The diminished 5th is resolved by falling a step. See (*a*), (*b*) and (*c*). The augmented 5th is resolved by rising a step. See (*d*). Obviously these discordant 5ths cannot be doubled.

7 RESOLUTIONS OF THE ROOT POSITIONS OF DIMINISHED AND AUGMENTED TRIADS. In addition to the melodic resolution of the discordant 5th the chords as a whole must resolve. The most common resolution of any discord is on to a chord whose root is a 4th higher. In accordance with this principle II moves to V, and III moves to VI. See Fig. 5 (*c*) and (*d*). But VII (major and minor key) does *not* move to III, except in a sequence. It sounds so like an incomplete ⁷V that it always moves to I. See Fig. 5 (*a*) and (*b*).

8 III*b* IN THE MINOR KEY. III*b* with the root at the top is used in place of V in a perfect or interrupted cadence, as in the major key. The 5th need not be prepared, as it is not discordant with the bass. The bass note must be doubled, as in the major key. See Fig. 6 (*a*) and (*b*).

Fig. 6 *a*) *b*)

**Exercise II.** Harmonise the following fragments, using a diminished or augmented triad in each case ; (*e*) is the only exercise in the major key.

Fig. 7 *a*) *b*) *c*)

**Exercise III.** Harmonise the following melodies :—

**Exercise IV.** Harmonise the following figured and un-figured basses :—

SUMMARY OF RULES AND CHORD PROGRESSIONS.

(1) Unusual triads may be freely used in the course of a sequence.

(2) Unusual triads sound satisfactory in a series of 1st inversions with the root at the top.

(3) III and III*b* in the major key sound satisfactory in the following progressions :—

(*a*) I III IV I with melody doh te lah soh.

(*b*) V III (or III*b*) VI.

(*c*) III*b* with the root at the top, before I or VI at a cadence. The bass note is doubled.

(4) Except in a sequence, the 5th of a diminished triad in root position is prepared, and resolves by falling a step ; the 5th of an augmented triad in root position is prepared, and resolves by rising a step.

(5)  II in the minor key resolves on to V.

III in the minor key resolves on to VI.

VII in the major and minor key resolves on to I, except in a sequence.

(6) III*b* in the minor key with the root at the top is used before I or VI at a cadence, as in the major key.

# CHAPTER III.

## SOME LESS COMMON USES OF 2nd INVERSIONS AND DOMINANT 7ths

1 THE AUXILIARY $^6_4$. A $^6_4$ can be produced by auxiliary notes. See Fig. 1. I and V can be decorated in this way. In an exercise with frequent chord changes the effect is rather halting, however, as there is no real change of chord for three beats.

Fig.1 *a)* *b)*

2 THE ARPEGGIO $^6_4$. If the bass moves in arpeggio, a $^6_4$ may be produced for the moment. See Fig. 2 (*a*). But such an idiom would be out of place in vocal exercises of the type you have been writing, it is more suitable for the piano. If the last note of the chord in the bass produces the $^6_4$, then it must move by step, as at (*b*) and (*c*).

Fig. 2 *a)* *b)* *c)*

3 THE PASSING $^6_4$. The passing $^6_4$ progression is occasionally found, using secondary triads. Fig. 3 shows examples in C

major. None of them are available in the minor. They would sound more effective if the accidentals marked in brackets were added, but these produce modulation, which you have not learnt.

4 UNUSUAL $\frac{6}{4}$ CHORDS. You will occasionally see a $\frac{6}{4}$ in an unusual position, but you will always find that the bass remains stationary or moves by step, and that in four part harmony the bass note is doubled. An unusual $\frac{6}{4}$ will probably have a " passing " effect, with the bass quitted by step, as at Fig. 4 (*a*) and (*b*). The bass of a $\frac{6}{4}$ *never* leaps.

**Exercise I.** Harmonise the following fragments, using a $\frac{6}{4}$ chord once in each case :—

5 IV*b* OR IV*c* BETWEEN TWO POSITIONS OF 7V. This is another " passing " effect. See Fig. 6. The bass and an upper part move in contrary motion by step, and an inversion of IV is used between two positions of 7V. Fah acts as a binding note, and resolves from the last position of 7V

Fig. 6 *a)*        *b)*        *c)*

6 IV*c* AFTER 7V AT A CADENCE. This is a natural combination of a dominant 7th and a cadential $\overset{6}{4}$, and you may have already used it. 7V | I ‖ decorated becomes 7V | IV*c* I ‖, and fah does not resolve until I is reached. See Fig. 7.

Fig. 7 *a)*        *b)*        *c)*

**Exercise II.** Harmonise the following fragments, using the dominant 7th at least once in each case :—

Fig. 8   *a)*        *b)*        *c)*

IV*c* I

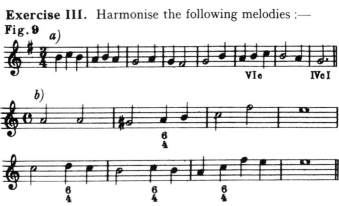

**Exercise III.** Harmonise the following melodies :—

**Fig. 9**

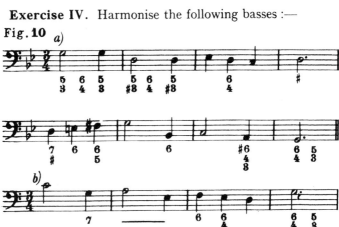

**Exercise IV.** Harmonise the following basses :—

**Fig. 10**

SUMMARY OF RULES AND CHORD PROGRESSIONS.

(1) An auxiliary $^6_4$ can decorate I and V.

(2) Movement in the bass can produce an arpeggio $^6_4$. If the last position of the chord is a $^6_4$, the bass must move by step.

(3) Passing $^6_4$s occasionally occur using secondary triads, and in unusual arrangements.

(4) The bass of a $^6_4$ should *never* leap.

(5) IV*b* and IV*c* can be used as passing chords between two positions of ⁷V. Fah resolves from the last position of ⁷V.

(6) IV*c* can come between ⁷V and I at a cadence. Fah does not resolve until I is reached.

## CHAPTER IV.

## MODULATION

(A thorough treatment of modulation is out of place in an elementary text book. This brief summary may, however, be useful to candidates who require it for examination purposes.)

1 RELATED KEYS. The most closely related keys to a given key centre are those which have the same signature, or whose signatures contain one sharp or flat more or less than the original signature.

From a major key centre :—

Dominant major ⟵ |Key centre| ⟶ Subdominant major

| | | |

Relative minor      Relative minor      Relative minor

(*i.e.*, Fah and soh major, ray me and lah minor).

From a minor key centre :—

Dominant minor ⟵ |Key centre| ⟶ Subdominant minor

| | | |

Relative major      Relative major      Relative major

(*i.e.*, Fah and soh minor, maw, law and taw major.)

**Exercise I.** Make a list of all the related keys from the following key centres : (1) C major ; (2) G minor ; (3) A♭ major ; (4) E minor ; (5) F♯ major.

2 PIVOT CHORD MODULATION. A " pivot " chord is a chord common to both keys, approached as if it belonged to the first key, and quitted as if it belonged to the second. See Fig. 1*.

**Fig. 1**

VI  VIb    Ic  ⁷V        I
    =IIb

Its most normal position is before V or Ic V at a cadence.

**Exercise II.** Harmonise the following. Use a pivot chord at *.

**Fig. 2**

*a)* G major to D major

*b)* D minor to F major

*c)* A minor to F major

*d)* E♭ major to G minor

**Exercise III.** Write four bar phrases, illustrating modulation by means of a pivot chord, from (a) F major to C major ; (b) B♭ major to G minor ; (c) E minor to A minor ; (d) A major to B minor ; (c) D minor to F major.

3 TRANSIENT MODULATION. Transient modulations (or "transitions") generally occur after I, and consist of ⁷V I (nearly always inverted) in the new key. There are frequently several in sequence. See Fig. 3.

**Fig. 3**

**Exercise IV.** Harmonise the following :—

**Exercise V.** By means of transient modulations (⁷V I) modulate from (*a*) C major through A minor, F major and D minor back to C major ; (*b*) E minor through C major, A minor and G major back to E minor.

4 KEY SCHEMES.

(1) The first few and last few bars must be in the tonic, in order to establish and re-establish the key.

(2) The chief cadence about half way through is generally in the dominant if the piece is major, and the relative major if the piece is minor. This modulation is normally by means of a pivot chord.

(3) Subsidiary modulations may occur elsewhere. They are generally on the sharp side of the key centre in the first half, and the flat side in the second half. They are normally transient, and the chords are nearly always inverted. Analyse Fig. 5 :—

Fig. 5

**Exercise VI.** Harmonise the following for S.A.T.B. :—

Fig. 6 a)

**Exercise VII.** Add another melody to the following :—

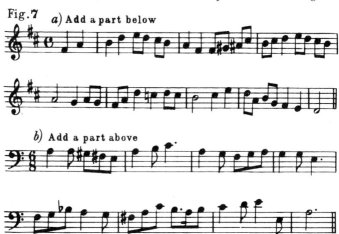

APPENDIX I

## RULES

(The Chapter in which the rule is first given is stated here, so that it can be referred to, if necessary. Tick each rule, as it is learnt.)

RANGE

Part II, Ch. III.

Keep within the following ranges :—

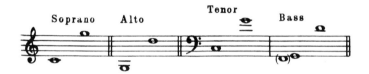

SPACING

Part II, Ch. III.

1. Do not have the tenor too low down, particularly if it is a 3rd from the bass.
2. Do not have more than an 8ve between adjacent voices, except between the bass and tenor.
3. Do not let the parts cross.

DOUBLING

Part II, Ch. III.

1. Root position.  Doubled root : good.
   Doubled 5th : possible.
   Doubled 3rd : generally poor.

Part II, Ch. X.

2. 1st inversions.  The 5th is frequently doubled, particularly when it is at the top.
3. Double the note which makes the smoothest progression.  Even the 3rd may occasionally be doubled when moving smoothly in contrary motion.

283

Part III, Ch. I.

    4. The 3rd of a secondary triad can be doubled more freely than the 3rd of a primary triad.

    5. In using V VI or VI V, double the 3rd in VI.

Part III, Ch. III.

    6. The 3rd is generally doubled in VII*b*.

Part IV, Ch. V.

    7. In four part writing, the bass note, *i.e.*, the 5th, of *all* $\frac{6}{4}$ chords is doubled, and the root and 3rd are each used once.

Part IV, Ch. VI.

    8. In four part writing $^7$V generally contains every note once, but occasionally the 5th is omitted and the root doubled.

OMITTING NOTES.

Part II, Ch. III

    1. The 5th can be omitted.

    2. The 3rd cannot be omitted.

Part IV, Ch. VI.

    3. The 5th can be omitted from the dominant 7th.

    4. The 3rd can very occasionally be omitted from the dominant 7th.

MELODIC MOVEMENT.

Part II, Ch. IV.

    1. Move smoothly, not often more than a 3rd in the inner parts.

    2. When there is a leap of more than a 4th, the next note should be inside the leap.

    3. 8ves are better than 6ths and 7ths in a melodic part.

    4. Te should almost always rise, and usually to doh. Exceptions :

        (*a*) It can move to lah when a part is moving doh te lah.

        (*b*) It can move to another note when V is repeated, but the last te must rise to doh.

Te should always rise to doh at a cadence.

5. Do not use an augmented interval—(fah te, major key).
6. If a diminished interval is used, the next note must be inside it.

Part II, Ch. IX.
7. The augmented intervals to avoid in the minor key are : (*a*) Maw te ; (*b*) fah te ; (*c*) law te ; (*d*) law ray.
8. Get some rhythmic variety in melodic parts, by turning repeated notes into one long note, or by moving to another position of the same chord, where it is correct and musical to do so. Do not move more quickly than the beat (until Part IV).

HARMONIC MOVEMENT.

Part II, Ch. V.
1. Do not overlap except (*a*) between two positions of the same chord ; (*b*) between tenor and bass at a perfect cadence when the tenor sings te doh.
2. Do not write consecutive 1sts, 5ths or 8ves.

Part II, Ch. VI.
3. Do not use exposed' 5ths and 8ves (outside parts) unless (*a*) the top part moves by step ; (*b*) between two positions of the same chord. (Primary triads.)

Part III, Ch. I.
4. Avoid exposed 5ths and 8ves when either or both chords concerned are secondary triads.

Part III, Ch. III.
5. A perfect and diminished 5th may follow each other, provided that they are not with the bass.

Part IV, Ch. II.
6. Decorations do not remedy faulty consecutives already present.
7. Decorations should not produce consecutive 5ths or 8ves on any part of adjacent beats, unless at least one note is unessential, and they are not next to each other.
8. Do not approach a unison by oblique motion.

Part IV, Ch. V.
9. Avoid consecutive perfect 4ths with the bass.

Part IV, Ch. VI.

10. Do not let a root and 7th move to or from an 8ve by similar motion.

SIMILAR CHORDS REPEATED HIGHER OR LOWER.

Part II, Ch. V.

1. Major key, IV and V. The 5th and 8ve must move in contrary motion to the bass.

Part II, Ch. IX.

2. Minor key, IV and V. The 3rd, as well as the 5th and 8ve must move in contrary motion to the bass, in order to avoid augmented intervals.

Part II, Ch. X.

3. Major key, IV*b* and V*b*. Double different notes.

Part II, Ch. XI.

4. Minor key, IV*b* and V*b*. Cannot be used, owing to the augmented interval in the bass.

Part III, Ch. I.

5. V VI and VI V. Double the 3rd in VI.

6. Consecutive 1st inversions. Place the root at the top, and double a different note in each chord.

FIGURED BASS.

Part II, Ch. XI.

1. Root position = $\binom{5}{3}$.

2. 1st inversion = $^{6}_{(3)}$.

3. Accidentals = ♯6 ; ♯(3).

Part IV, Ch. IV.

4. Decorations over a figured bass are generally indicated by figures. A line under moving bass notes indicates that the chord is unchanged.

Part IV, Ch. V.

5. A second inversion is figured $^{6}_{4}$. When a root position on the same bass note follows, it is figured $^{5}_{3}$.

Part IV, Ch. VI.

6. $^{7}V = \left\{ \begin{smallmatrix} 7 \\ (5) \\ (3) \end{smallmatrix} \right.$ ; $^{7}Vb = \left\{ \begin{smallmatrix} 6 \\ 5 \\ (3) \end{smallmatrix} \right.$ ; $^{7}Vc = \left\{ \begin{smallmatrix} (6) \\ 4 \\ 3 \end{smallmatrix} \right.$ ; $^{7}Vd = \left\{ \begin{smallmatrix} (6) \\ 4 \\ 2 \end{smallmatrix} \right.$

Figures in brackets are generally implied.

TWO PART WRITING.

## TWO PART WRITING.

**Part III, Ch. V.**

1. Each part must be interesting, have a good curve, and if possible a climax.
2. The parts must be as contrasted as possible. Use plenty of contrary motion.
3. Perfect concords should be used sparingly. They are good :—
    (*a*) At the beginning and the end ;
    (*b*) Before or after another position of the same chord ;
    (*c*) Used smoothly and approached by contrary motion ;
    (*d*) Approached by similar motion between primary triads, if the top part moves by step.

    Use them on a weak beat in preference to a strong one.
4. Use plenty of imperfect concords, but do not write a string of consecutive 3rds and 6ths.
5. The two parts must imply good harmony.
6. Imitation and sequence are useful devices for creating interest.

**Part IV, Ch. II.**

7. Aim for rhythmic contrast between the parts. Use occasional rests, and let the parts imitate each other.

DECORATION (MELODIC).

**Part IV, Ch. I.**

1. Decoration can consist of essential and unessential notes.
2. Essential notes are chord notes, whether concords or discords.
3. Unessential notes do not belong to the chord. There are four main types :—
    (*a*) *Passing Notes*, (accented or unaccented), which must move by step in the same direction, from chord to chord note.
    (*b*) *Auxiliary Notes*, (accented and unaccented), which are the notes above and below the chord

note. They are used in the following figures :
(1) Mordent : (2) lower mordent ; (3) turn ;
(4) changing note ; (5) an auxiliary note between two chord notes a step apart ; (6) an
auxiliary note approached by leap ; (7) appoggiatura ; (8) acciaccatura.

(c) *Suspensions,* which occur on the accent and are
approached from the same note in the previous
chord, afterwards falling (occasionally rising) by
step to the next chord note.

(d) *Anticipations,* which occur off the accent, and
anticipate a chord note over the previous chord,
being then repeated as their chord is sounded.

Part IV, Ch. II.

4. Essential notes must occur on the accent (at present).

5. Essential, passing or auxiliary notes may occur in
between the accents. Use passing and auxiliary notes
in preference to essential notes, as they produce a
smoother part.

6. In dotted figures use an essential note against the dot.

7. Two parts can only make decorations at the same time
if (a) both are essential ; or (b) both are unessential
and (1) proceed in consecutive 3rds or 6ths, or (2)
sound an 8ve by contrary conjunct motion.

Part IV, Ch. IV.

8. Two decorations occurring at the same time must have
the same rhythm (at present).

9. Decorations must not be written in more than two
parts at once (at present).

MELODIC MINOR. *Unessential Use.*

Part IV, Ch. III.

1. The following idioms employing the melodic minor
can be used :—

(1) *Soh* lah te *doh* ⎫ Two passing notes between
(2) *Doh* taw law *soh* ⎭ essential notes.
(3) *Soh* lah *te,* and *te* lah *soh* ⎰ One passing note
(4) *Doh* taw *law* and ⎰ between essential
      *law* taw *doh* ⎱ notes.

(5) *Law* taw *law* ⎫ Auxiliary note between essen-
(6) *Te* lah *te*    ⎭ tial notes.
    The essential notes are in italics.

## Essential Use.

Part V, Ch. I.

2. The melodic minor is used essentially when a melodic part moves lah te or taw law.
3. Use any concords which result from the melodic minor, and which form good progressions.
4. Consecutive 1st inversions employing the melodic minor are common.
5. Do not double lah. Taw can be doubled if one part is following the scale line.
6. Use te in the next chord but one after taw.

### SECOND INVERSIONS.

Part IV, Ch. V.

1. All 2nd inversions are discords, and must only be used under special conditions.
2. 2nd inversions are decorative chords.
3. A cadential $\frac{6}{4}$ resolves on to a root position on the same bass note. The progressions which can be used thus are I*c* V and IV*c* I.
4. A cadential $\frac{6}{4}$ must occur on a stronger accent than its resolution.
5. In deciding what chords can be used before a cadential $\frac{6}{4}$, imagine the progression without the $\frac{6}{4}$.
6. The use of cadential $\frac{6}{4}$s sometimes creates feminine endings.
7. A passing $\frac{6}{4}$ can occur when the melody is d r m, m r d, f s l or l s f (and the equivalent in the minor key) and the bass has the same notes in the reverse order.
8. A passing $\frac{6}{4}$ occurs on a weak accent.
9. Consecutive 2nd inversions can occur in the progression I*b* V*c* | IV*c* I ‖, and in no other.

Part V, Ch. VI.

10. I*c* can resolve on to $^7$V or $^7$V*d* at a cadence.

Part V, Ch. III.

11. An auxiliary $\frac{6}{4}$ can decorate I and V.

12. Movement in the bass can produce an arpeggio ⁶₄. If the last position of the chord is a ⁶₄, the bass must move by step.

13. Passing ⁶₄s occasionally occur using secondary triads, and in unusual arrangements.

14. The bass of a ⁶₄ should *never* leap.

15. IV*c* can be used as a passing chord between two positions of ⁷V.

16. IV*c* can come between ⁷V and I at a cadence.

DOMINANT SEVENTHS

Part IV, Ch. VI.

1. In ⁷V fah normally falls to me (or maw) and te rises to doh. Fah rises, however, in moving from ⁷V*c* to I*b*.

2. The resolutions of ⁷V are as follows : ⁷V to I or VI ; ⁷V*b* to I ; ⁷V*c* to I or I*b* (irregular resolution) ; ⁷V*d* to I*b*.

3. ⁷V*c* is used as a passing chord between I and I*b*, particularly when the melody is me fah soh, or soh fah me (and the equivalent in the minor key).

4. ⁷V can be resolved ornamentally.

5. When ⁷V moves from one position to another, the last position must resolve correctly.

6. ⁷V can be used in place of V.
   ⁷V*b* can be used in place of V*b*.
   ⁷V*c* can be used in place of V*c* or VII*b*.
   ⁷V*d* can be used in place of V.

7. I*c* can resolve on to ⁷V or ⁷V*d* at a cadence.

8. ⁷V and its·inversions are frequently used at the beginning, middle and ends of phrases. Remember that fah can be harmonised by this chord, as well as soh, te and ray.

Part V, Ch. III.

9. IV*b* and IV*c* can be used as passing chords between two positions of ⁷V. Fah resolves from the last position of ⁷V.

10. IV*c* can come between ⁷V and I at a cadence. Fah does not resolve until I is reached.

III AND III*b* MAJOR KEY. DIMINISHED AND AUGMENTED
TRIADS.

Part V, Ch. II.

1. Unusual triads may be freely used in the course of a sequence.

2. Unusual triads sound satisfactory in a series of 1st inversions, with the root at the top.

3. III and III*b* in the major key sound satisfactory in the following progressions :—

   (*a*) I III IV I with melody doh te lah soh.

   (*b*) V III (or III*b*) VI.

   (*c*) III*b* with the root at the top, before I or VI at a cadence. The bass note must be doubled.

4. Except in a sequence, the 5th of a diminished triad is prepared, and resolves by falling a step ; the 5th of an augmented triad is prepared, and resolves by rising a step.

5. II in the minor key resolves on to V.

   III in the minor key resolves on to VI.

   VII in the major and minor key resolves on to I.

6. III*b* in the minor key with the root at the top is used before I or VI at a cadence, as in the major key.

# HARMONIC PROGRESSIONS

## PRINCIPLES OF CHORD CHOICE.

Part II, Ch. VI.

1. The same chord should not be used ᴜ—. It is good —ᴜ.
2. The final cadence chord should not be used on the previous strong accent.
3. Avoid harmonising doh with I on an accent, except for the final chord or (occasionally) on the first strong accent.

Part II, Ch. X.

4. Do not use the same chord ᴜ— even if one position is inverted.
5. Outside parts should move mostly in contrary motion or in consecutive 3rds and 6ths. 3rds and 6ths between melody and bass sound softer than 5ths and 8ves.
6. Do not generally move further than a 3rd from the bass of a first inversion.
7. An inverted cadence is good at the end of a subordinate phrase.
8. Inverted chords are often good at the beginning of a phrase.

Part III, Ch. I.

9. Roots moving a 4th or 5th are good when both chords are in root position or where one chord is inverted.
10. Roots moving a 3rd, both chords being root positions, are good when falling and poor when rising. If either or both chords are inverted, both progressions are awkward to manage and are rather rare. Chords having two notes in common are better —ᴜ.
11. Roots moving a 2nd are always awkward to manage and rarely good. IV V and V VI are the best of these progressions. If both chords are inverted the effect

is always good, provided that a different note is doubled in each chord. The root is generally in the melody.

12. Establish the key clearly at the beginnings and ends of phrases.

Part IV, Ch. II.

13. The chord rhythm must be recognised before an exercise is worked.

Part IV, Ch. VI.

14. The same bass note can be used ∪— if the second note is the 7th of a new chord.

Part V, Ch. II.

15. Unusual triads may be freely used in the course of a sequence.

16. Unusual triads sound satisfactory in a series of 1st inversions with the root at the top.

### CHOICE OF MELODY NOTE.

Part II, Ch. VII.

1. Use plenty of 3rds from the bass in the melody, particularly on the accent, as they are a little softer than 5ths and 8ves.

2. Move smoothly in the melody but not too much round the same notes. Get a good melodic line, with a climax, if possible.

3. Avoid doh as the melody note over I on a strong accent, except for the final chord, or (occasionally) on the first strong accent.

Part II, Ch. X.

4. The root sounds well as the melody note of a first inversion ; the 5th is quite good ; the 3rd is occasionally used when moving smoothly by contrary motion.

Part III, Ch. III.

5. It is generally best to have the root at the top of the 1st inversion of a secondary triad. VII*b* frequently has the 3rd at the top, however.

COMMON PROGRESSIONS, WITH EXAMPLES.

Part II. Ch. X. **1.** Two positions of the same chord moving — ∪ 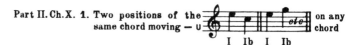 on any chord

I   Ib   I   Ib

**2.** An inversion moving up a 2nd or 3rd to a root position, the melody moving in contrary motion and making the intervals 6 3 with the bass. Also good backwards.  and on other chords

Ib   IV   Ib   V

**3.** Ib IV and Vb I with melody and bass moving in consecutive 3rds. Also good backwards.

Ib   IV   Vb   I

**4.** IVb Vb I, major key only. (or melodic minor).

IVb Vb   I   IVb Vb   I

Part III. Ch. I. **5.** II to V, Vb or VI.

II   V   II   V   II Vb  I   II   VI   II   VI

**6.** IV, V or VI to II.

IV   II   V   V ꞏII   VI   VI   II   V

**7.** V, I or II to VI.

V   VI   I  VI   I   VI   II   VI   II   VI

**8.** VI to V, IV or II.

VI   V   VI   IV   VI   II

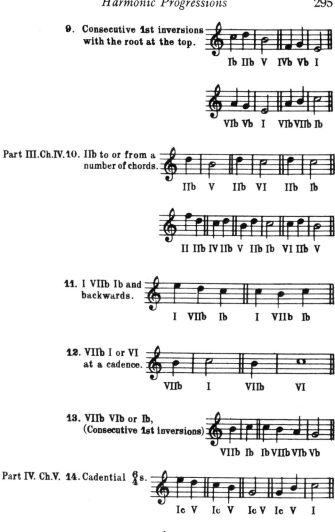

**9.** Consecutive **1st** inversions with the root at the top.

Ib  IIb  V  IVb  Vb  I

VIb  Vb  I  VIb VIIb Ib

Part III.Ch.IV.**10.** IIb to or from a number of chords.

IIb  V  IIb  VI  IIb  Ib

II  IIb IV IIb  V  IIb Ib  VI IIb  V

**11.** I VIIb Ib and backwards.

I  VIIb  Ib  I  VIIb  Ib

**12.** VIIb I or VI at a cadence.

VIIb  I  VIIb  VI

**13.** VIIb VIb or Ib, (Consecutive **1st** inversions)

VIIb Ib  Ib VIIb VIb Vb

Part IV. Ch.V. **14.** Cadential $^6_4$s.

Ic V  Ic V  Ic V  Ic V  I

V  IVc I  IVc I  IVc I

**15.** Passing $^6_4$s.

I Vc Ib    Ib Vc I    IVb Ic IV IV Ic IVb

Part IV. Ch.VI. **16.** $^7$V.

$^7$V    I    $^7$V    I    $^7$V    VI    $^7$V    I

**17.** Inversions of $^7$V.

$^7$Vb    I    $^7$Vb    I    I $^7$Vc    Ib

Ib$^7$Vc I    $^7$Vc Ib    $^7$Vd    Ib    $^7$Vd    Ib

## CADENCE PROGRESSIONS.

Perfect  V  I.

Plagal  IV  I.

Imperfect.  Any chord that leads well to V.

Interrupted.  V VI (or any other unexpected chord.)

*Inverted Cadences.*

Perfect  (1) V*b*  I ; (2)  V  I*b* ; (3)  $^7$V*b*  I ; (4)  $^7$V*c*  I ; (5)
    $^7$V*c*  I*b* ; (6)  $^7$V*d*  I*b*.

Plagal.  (1) IV*b*  I ; (2)  IV  I*b*.

Imperfect.  Either chord inverted.

Interrupted.  V*b*  VI.

Other possible cadences are :—

(*a*)  I (or I*b*) IV, a kind of imperfect cadence.

(*b*)  VII*b* I or I*b*, a kind of perfect cadence.

(*c*)  III*b* I, a kind of perfect cadence.

*Chords to use before V or $^7$V in perfect, imperfect and inter-*
*rupted cadences.*

I.    Good if V does not move to I.

I*b*.    Good if V does not move to I.

II.    Very good.

II*b*.    Very good.

IV.    Very good.

IV*b*.   Good.
 V*b*.   Good if —ᴗ.
VI.   Good if V does not lead to VI.
I*c* can come between all the above chords (except V*b* and V.)
*Chords to use before IV in a plagal cadence.*
 I*b*.   Good.
IV*b*.   Good if —ᴗ.
 V.   Possible if melody moves ray fah.
VI.   Very good.

PROGRESSIONS TO AVOID OR USE SPARINGLY.

Part II, Ch. VI.
   1. Avoid using V IV unless the melody is ray fah.
Part II, Ch. X.
   2. V*b* cannot move to IV.
   3. Do not generally move further than a 3rd from the
       bass of a first inversion.
Part II, Ch. XI.
   4. IV*b* and V*b* cannot be used next to each other in the
       minor key (until Part V).
Part III, Ch. II.
   5. II cannot be used in the minor key (until Part V.)
Part III, Ch. III.
   6. The bass of VI*b* generally moves by step, except when
       moving to its own root position.  It can move to II,
       V*b*, VII*b* or VI.  Use it sparingly.
Part III, Ch. IV.
   7. II*b* cannot move to II (until part V) and rarely moves
       to VI, in the minor key.
   8. VI*b* is rare in the minor key.  V*b* and VI are the best
       chords to use next to it.
   9. VII*b* cannot move to VI or VI*b* in the minor key
       (until part V.)
Part V, Ch. II.
   10. III and III*b*, major key, and diminished and aug-
       mented triads should be used sparingly. (See separate
       rules.)

## METHODS OF WORKING

METHOD OF HARMONISING A MELODY IN FOUR PARTS.

1. Sing the melody to sol-fa.
2. If there is more than one phrase add the phrase marks, and work a phrase at a time.
3. Decide on the cadence chords ; write the Roman numerals and bass.
4. Start at the beginning and choose the chords, writing the Roman numerals and bass. (See " Choice of chords " in appendix.)

   Think in progressions rather than in isolated chords. Put in common progressions that you recognise first, then fill in the gaps. (In early stages it may be wise to write down the names of *all* the chords which are possible for a melody note, and then decide between them.)
5. Sing the bass to sol-fa and check it. (See " Melodic Movement ", and " Choice of bass note ".)
6. Try to hear melody and bass together. Check them. Look for exposed or consecutive 5ths and 8ves by naming the intervals throughout.
7. Write down any comments which will help in working, such as (*a*) " te " (and its name if a minor key) ; (*b*) a " x " (warning to move contrary to the bass where the bass moves by step, both notes requiring root positions or both 1st inversions) ; (*c*) " two 3rds " over VI when before or after V ; (*d*) the names of notes requiring resolution, as in the dominant 7th, augmented and diminished triads.

*Filling In.*
1. Fill in the first chord.
2. Fill in the second chord, moving as smoothly as possible, and contrary to the bass where there is a " x".

*Checking.*

As soon as each chord is written check immediately, using your ear as much as possible. Check : —

1. Each separate chord for range, spacing, doubling, and omitting notes (see rules).
2. Melodic movement (see rules). Sing to sol-fa.
3. Harmonic movement (see rules).
4. Resolutions of discords (see rules).

*Continuation.*

Continue with the next chord in the same way. When you have come to the end try to hear the final result. Then sing the exercise in parts if you are in class. If you are alone, try it through on the piano.

*Note.*—Checking will gradually become quick and automatic, so that you can see at a glance that the progression looks right. Also you will not need all the " reminders " as time goes on. But never omit trying to hear what you have written.

METHOD OF HARMONISING A BASS IN FOUR PARTS.

1. Sing the bass to sol-fa.
2. If there is more than one phrase add the phrase marks and work a phrase at a time.
3. Decide on the cadence chords ; write the Roman numerals.
4. Start at the beginning and choose the chords, writing the Roman numerals. (See " Choice of chords " in Appendix.) Put in common progressions that you recognise first, then fill in the gaps. You may find it convenient to write parts of the melody at the same time.
5. Fill in the melody. Choose notes which give a good line, with a climax if possible ; move contrary to the bass or in consecutive 3rds and 6ths with it most of the time.
6. Sing the melody to sol-fa and check it. (See " Melodic Movement " and " Choice of melody note ".)
7. Try to hear the melody and bass together. Check them. Look for exposed and consecutive 5ths and 8ves by naming the intervals wherever there is similar motion.
8. Write down any helpful comments you may require. Then fill in and check, as in harmonising a melody.

METHOD OF ADDING ONE MELODY TO ANOTHER.

1. Sing the given melody to sol-fa.
2. Add the phrase marks.
3. Choose a chord scheme. It can be modified later, if necessary.
4. From the chord scheme write the added part. Aim at the following :—
   (*a*) Smooth movement and a good melodic line. At every move try first for stepwise movement (with or without decoration), before thinking of other possibilities.
   (*b*) Contrary motion between the two parts as much as possible.
   (*c*) Essential notes on the accents. Essential, passing or auxiliary notes, as decorations, in between the accents.
   (*d*) Imperfect in preference to perfect concords on the strong accents.
   (*e*) Rhythmic contrast between the parts, if possible.
   When doubtful about a passage, leave a gap, and fill it in afterwards.
5. Sing the added part to sol-fa and check it.
6. Try to hear the two parts together. Check them.
7. Play or sing the final result.

APPENDIX IV

## MISCELLANEOUS EXERCISES

1. Analyse the harmony of the following passages :—

2. Point out the errors in the following passages :—

*a)*

*b)*

3. Complete the following exercises by inserting the stated chords in the numbered spaces :—

    (*a*) (1) 1st inversion tonic ; (2) root position mediant ; (3) a cadential $^6_4$ ; (4) its resolution ; (5) root position submediant.

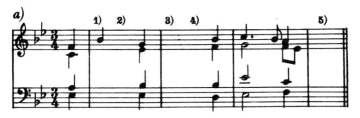

(b) (1) An inversion of the dominant 7th; (2) a cadential ♯₄; (3) an inversion of the dominant 7th; (4) and (5) two chords using the melodic minor; (6) root position supertonic.

4. Complete the following exercise by placing appropriate chords in the empty spaces :—

5. Write progressions of four chords, ending with the following cadences : (*a*) perfect in B♭ major ; (*b*) interrupted in G minor ; (*c*) plagal in F major.

6. Write progressions of three chords introducing (*a*) the root position of the supertonic triad in E minor ; (*b*) the 1st inversion of the triad on the leading note in A♭ major ; (*c*) the root position of the mediant triad in E major.

7. Write the following progressions in four part harmony :—
    (*a*) 1st inversion of the supertonic ; 2nd inversion of the tonic ; last inversion of the dominant 7th ; 1st inversion of the tonic, in F minor.
    (*b*) Root position of the submediant ; root position of the subdominant ; root position of the supertonic ; 1st inversion of the dominant 7th, and its resolution, in A major.

8. Resolve the following chords : (*f*), (*g*) and (*h*) should be resolved in two ways each.

9. Write out the dominant 7th and its inversions in A♭ major, and give one resolution of each position.

10. Write out and resolve all the discordant triads in E minor.

11. Harmonise the following progressions :—

*a)*

*b)*

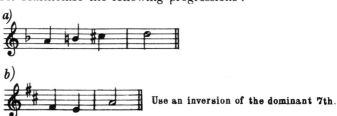

Use an inversion of the dominant 7th.

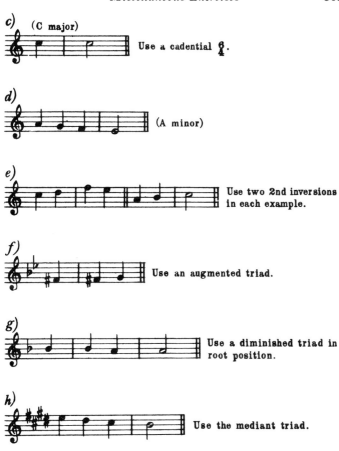

c) (C major)

Use a cadential ⁶₄.

d)

(A minor)

e)

Use two 2nd inversions in each example.

f)

Use an augmented triad.

g)

Use a diminished triad in root position.

h)

Use the mediant triad.

i)

## SOME ADDITIONAL RUDIMENTS OF MUSIC

1 NOTE LENGTHS. The following table shows the comparative lengths of notes, giving their time-names and their shorthand when the crotchet is the beat.

| Number of beats | Name of Note | Sign | Time-name | Short-hand |
|---|---|---|---|---|
| 8 | Breve | 𝄂o𝄂 | rarely used when ♩ is the beat | |
| 4 | Semibreve | o | Taa-aa-aa-aa | ℍℿℿ |
| 3 | Dotted Minim | ♩. | Taa-aa-aa | ℿ |
| 2 | Minim | ♩ | Taa-aa | ℎ |
| 1 | Crotchet | ♩ | Taa | I |
| ½ | Quavers | ♪, ♫ | Ta-te | ↳ |
| ¼ | Semiquavers | ♬, ♬ | Ta-fa-te-fe | W |
| ⅛ | Demisemiquaver | ♪ | — | — |
| ¹⁄₁₆ | Semidemisemiquaver | ♪ | — | — |

A dot after a note or rest makes it half as long again. A second dot adds half the value of the previous dot, and so on.

2 CORRESPONDING RESTS

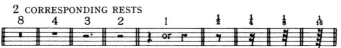

Rests are normally written in the third space. A semibreve rest is always used for a whole bar except where it might confuse because it could also represent part of a bar, as e.g. in $\frac{3}{2}$ or $\frac{4}{2}$ time.

3 SOME COMMONLY USED TIME PATTERNS IN SIMPLE TIME, WITH THEIR TIME-NAMES AND THEIR SHORTHAND WHEN ♩ IS THE BEAT.

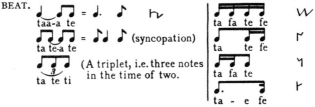

**4** SIMPLE TIME SIGNATURES. The top figure states the number of beats in the bar. The bottom figure states the kind of note used for the beat, in fractions of a semibreve., e.g :—

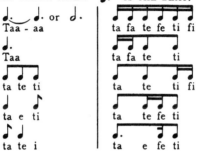

**5** COMPOUND TIME. In simple time the beats are written as undotted notes (e.g. crotchets) and divide into two. In compound time the beats are written as dotted notes so that they may divide into three equal parts, e.g. can divide into , into etc.

**6** SOME COMMONLY USED TIME PATTERNS IN COMPOUND TIME, WITH THEIR TIME-NAMES WHEN IS THE BEAT.

**7.** COMPOUND TIME SIGNATURES. A dotted note cannot be expressed as a simple fraction of a semibreve. So the next lowest note value is used in a compound time signature, e.g.

N.B. $\frac{6}{8}$ is *not* 6 quaver beats, but 2 dotted crotchet beats. $\frac{6}{8}$, $\frac{9}{8}$, and $\frac{12}{8}$ correspond to $\frac{2}{4}$, $\frac{3}{4}$, and $\frac{4}{4}$ in simple time.

**8** GROUPING OF NOTE VALUES. Notes belonging to the same beat are normally grouped together, e.g.

But the complete first half or second half of a bar in quadruple time may have all the notes grouped together if they are of the same length, e.g. But not

♩ ♫♫ ‖ Similarly, notes of the same length may be grouped together for a whole bar, e.g. **¾** ♫♫♫ ‖

Rests are treated similarly, e.g. **⁴⁄₄** ♩ ♪ ‿ ‖   **⁴⁄₄** ♪↷↿↿↾·♪‖

but not **⁴⁄₄** ♩ ‿ ♩ ‖

If words are used, then notes belonging to the same *syllable* (not word) are grouped together, e.g. ♫ ♩  ♪ ♫
blue sky, cloud-y sky

9 BARRING. When adding bar lines to a melody, try to hear it mentally and feel where the accents come. It must be so barred that the note groupings and rests are correct, and that a long note or a dotted note does not spread over a bar line.

10 CLEFS. In the middle ages the monks used a great stave of eleven lines, sufficient to cover the notes used by all voices from treble to bass. As, however, five were sufficient for any one type of voice, the particular five required were chosen from the eleven, with a C, G or F shown as a key (clef in French) to the others.

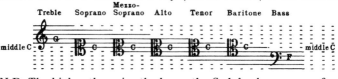

N.B. The higher the voice the lower the C clef, when seen on five lines in isolation, e.g.

Nowadays the alto clef is used mainly for the viola, while the tenor clef is used for the tenor trombone and the higher notes of the 'cello and the bassoon. The other C clefs are rarely used.

11 CHROMATIC SCALE. The harmonic chromatic scale (used for chromatic chords) consists of one tonic and one dominant and two of all other notes, e.g. Key of C

The melodic chromatic scale (used for melodic decoration involving unessential notes) consists of one mediant and one leading note ascending and is the same as the harmonic chromatic descending, e.g. Key of C

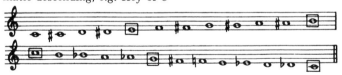

12 THE MOST COMMONLY USED ORNAMENTS.

The speed at which these ornaments are performed and the number of repetitions in a trill depend upon the speed of the music.

13 ITALIAN MUSICAL TERMS IN GENERAL USE

**SPEED**

*Grave.* Very slow and solemn
*Largo.* Very slow and broad
*Adagio.* Slow, at ease
*Lento.* Slow
*Andante.* Rather slow, walking pace
*Moderato.* Moderate speed
*Allegretto.* Rather quick
*Allegro.* Quick
*Vivace.* With life
*Presto.* Very quick
*Prestissimo.* As quickly as possible

**MODIFICATIONS OF SPEED**

*Accelerando* (*Accel.*). Accelerating

*Rallentando* (*Rall.*). ⎫ Getting
*Ritardando* (*Rit.*) ⎬ slower
*Ritenuto* (*Rit.*) ⎭
*Allargando.* Broadening, more like largo
*A tempo.* ⎫ Back to original
*Tempo Primo.* ⎭ speed
*Meno mosso.* Less moved, slower
*Piu mosso.* More moved, quicker

**INTENSITY**

*Fortissimo* (*ff*). As loudly as possible.
*Forte,* (*f*). Loud
*Mezzo forte* (*mf*). Moderately loud
*Mezzo piano* (*mp*). Moderately soft

*Piano, (p.)* Soft
*Pianissimo, (pp)*. As softly as
possible.

MODIFICATIONS OF INTENSITY

*Crescendo, Cresc.* (◁) getting
gradually louder
*Decrescendo, Decresc.* (▷) Getting gradually softer
*Diminuendo, Dim.* (▷), Getting gradually softer
*Sforzando (sf)* Strong accent

EXPRESSION
*Affetuoso.* Affectionately
*Agitato.* Agitated
*Animato.* Animated
*Arco.* With the bow (string
instruments)
*Assai.* Very much
*Brillante.* Brilliantly
*Cantabile.* In a singing style
*Con brio.* With vigour
*Con fuoco.* With fire.
*Con ped.* With the pedal
*Con sordino.* Muted
*Da Capo (D.C.).* From the
beginning
*Dal Segno, (D.S.)* Back to the
sign 𝄋.

*Dolce.* Sweetly
*Espressivo.* With expression
*Fine.* The end
*Grazioso.* Gracefully
*Legato.* Smoothly
*Leggiero.* Lightly
*Maestoso.* Majestically
*Marcato.* Marked
*M.M.* ♩=60. Maelziel's Metro-
nome at ♩=60, i.e. to tick
60 times a minute.
*Molto.* Much
*Pesante.* Heavily
*Pizzicato.* Plucked (string insts.)
*Poco a poco.* Little by little.
*Scherzando.* Playfully
*Sempre.* Always
*Sostenuto.* Sustained
*Sotto voce.* Under the voice,
softly
*Staccato.* Detached.
*Subito.* Suddenly
*Tenuto.* Held
*Tre corde.* Use three strings of
piano, i.e. release soft pedal
*Troppo.* Too much
*Tutti.* All the performers
*Una corda.* Use one string of
piano, i.e. soft pedal
*Vivo.* Lively

**14** SIGNS AND ABBREVIATIONS.

 End of a section; with repeat mark

𝄎. Repeat the note at ♪ speed

 Alternate the two notes at ♪ speed

𝄐 Pause

G.P. General Pause (all performers)

8va An octave higher

Con. 8 Play in octaves

    Tie.  Do not repeat the note

Slur.  Play as legato as possible

staccato

very staccato

Just separated from each other

M.D.    Main droite.  Right Hand
M.G.    Main gauche.  Left hand
V.S.    Volti subito.  Turn over quickly.

# INDEX

312